Crossing the Threshold

Female Officers
and
Police-Perpetrated Domestic Violence

Diane Wetendorf

Diane Wetendorf, Inc.
Breaking our isolation
Confronting the system
Educating our community

Crossing the Threshold: Female Officers and Police-Perpetrated Domestic Violence
Diane Wetendorf

Copyright ©2006 by Diane Wetendorf, Inc.
Second printing, 2007.

Printed in the United States of America. All rights reserved. No part of this book may be reproduced or transmitted in any form without prior written permission from the author and publisher.

Published by Diane Wetendorf, Inc.
126 E. Wing St., Suite 141
Arlington Heights, IL 60004
(847) 749-2560
E-mail: dwetendorf@dwetendorf.com
http://www.abuseofpower.info

For information regarding quantity or institutional discounts, please contact Diane Wetendorf, Inc. at (847) 749-2560 or dwetendorf@dwetendorf.com.

Cover and book design by Carolyn Hankett, M.B.A.
Cover art inspired by Leanor Boulin Johnson, Ph.D.

Library of Congress Control Number: 2006906923
Wetendorf, Diane
Crossing the Threshold: Female Officers and Police-Perpetrated Domestic Violence/Diane Wetendorf.
Includes bibliographic references.
1. Policewomen. 2. Family violence. 3. Sex discrimination in employment. 4. Police misconduct.
ISBN 978-1-933556-48-2

Officer and victim quotes are derived from published research,[1] public documents,[2] court testimony, interviews and personal correspondence with the author. Identifying information, such as names, dates and locations have been changed to protect our correspondents.

Printed and bound by Publishers' Graphics, LLC.

For personal or professional reasons, the majority of the women who contributed to this book have asked to remain anonymous. In struggling with my decision whether to name those who did not request anonymity, I have again come to appreciate that until every woman can openly speak her truth without fear, the freedom of all women is in jeopardy. I decided to err on the side of caution by refraining from publicly identifying any of the contributors.

To all of you who had the courage to share your personal stories and your professional experiences, I thank you from the bottom of my heart for trusting me to record your history. Please know that by telling your own truth you are reaching out to help your sisters cross their own thresholds to truth and power. Kiss yourselves sweetly—you've done a very good thing.

Thank you to all of the officers and civilians who reviewed the manuscript and gave your insights and encouragement.

I dedicate this book to Carrie Hankett, without whose love, patience, determination and talents the book would not have come to be. Carrie's dedication of countless hours and limitless energy has been beyond measure—her spirit is present in every page of the book you hold in your hands. Thank you, Carrie, from all of us.

Contents

Prologue vii
Author's Note ix
Introduction 1
Historical, Social and Cultural Context 7
The Police Culture 27
Police Domestic Violence on the Radar 57
He's the "Victim" 83
Network of Power 93
Advocates in the Network 121
Crossing the Threshold 129
In Honor of Those Silenced 139
References 140
Endnotes 147
About the Author 154
Selected Publications 155

Prologue

Set aside your training, your engrained, reactionary, "within seconds respond and make a decision" mentality. Look through all of that to your inner core. Allow your recollections of words shared as you pass by in a hallway, at home or at work float back to the forefront. Remember words and inflection exchanged as you sit car-to-car, or as you sit on a perimeter for hours on end. Let those words speak to you again.

Recall the volumes of shared statements spoken only through a glance—let them speak to you again. Hear that bold statement of visual communication as it sinks in. Put down the ramming shield, your protective armor just far enough to let the unjaded, child-like levels of awareness be heard. For these are the moments we are truest to ourselves, truest to our souls. As you read, give this gift to yourself. It is something no one can take from you. It is okay to say, "Oh, my God, that's me." No one will hear that as you read silently, to yourself, in your head.

The only true badge of courage that any of us can wear is one that is legitimized once the truth is acknowledged—*Our* truth is acknowledged as fact, as reality. This is the single, untarnished shield that exists. Wear this badge of courage proudly.

To have acknowledged and embraced the truth brings inner peace, acceptance, forgiveness, and the ability to forge ahead, to mark change. In turn, you honor your oath of service to your community, to your profession, to your badge, and most importantly, to yourself.

Cmdr. Krista Osborne, Ph.D. (Retired)

Author's Note

I have listened to the stories of thousands of victims of police-perpetrated domestic violence over the last twenty years in my capacity as counselor, consultant and advocate. Many of these victims are or have been police officers themselves. Though each woman who experiences abuse in an intimate relationship is a unique individual with her own unique experience, there are many more similarities than differences in the stories the women tell. When I have written about these women's experiences, other women tell me, "That is the story of my life. It's like you were inside my living room or bedroom recording the things he said to me." Most women tell me that until they read my writing, they'd felt utterly alone.

The feedback and validation that I have received has encouraged me to continue writing. I have chosen to focus this particular book on female police officers because their experiences go right to the heart of the matter of police-perpetrated violence. Their stories pretty much tell it all. The fact that most of them have requested that I not publicly acknowledge or thank them for their contributions to this book reveals the power of the taboo against their sharing their stories. Some of them are still police officers, others have lost their careers—none of them can safely speak the truth of their lives publicly for fear of the potential consequences.

It is not my intention to offend individual male police officers who are not batterers, nor is it my intention to incriminate all police departments. I am not painting all officers with the same brush and I ask the reader to keep in mind that I am talking about *officers who batter,* not all officers. I think it is insulting to praise those who do *not* batter their intimate partners and those who hold batterers accountable; that is simply their moral and professional obligation as human beings and as officers.

I hope that all who read this will find something of value in my writing, and that, above all, it rings true to the experiences of female officers. I hope to increase the understanding and empathy of the officers' colleagues, supervisors, family members, friends and the public so that we all are able to validate and support the officers and hold perpetrators accountable. We cannot afford not to tell the truth for fear of offending the "Powers-That-Be." The time has come to speak the truth to power.

Diane Wetendorf

Introduction

It is always a volatile situation when a police officer is the perpetrator of domestic violence; it is an explosive situation when both the perpetrator and the victim are officers. Fully comprehending the dynamics of the situation takes more than understanding "Domestic Violence 101." It requires understanding how completely males dominate the profession of policing, and how they have used the institution and culture of policing to preserve and protect male dominance both within the profession of policing and within larger society.

What is different about this book is that it examines how male police officers' institutional power within society and within the police ranks filters down into the intimate relationships of police officers, and why the institution has historically ignored or denied police-perpetrated violence against women. We will begin with a brief look at the history of policing, concentrating on how the profession has treated black and female officers. Next, we will explore the institution of policing—its culture and how individuals are indoctrinated, accepted or rejected based on their acceptance of the culture. With such background, we will finally look at domestic violence in the ranks, exploring how the players in the criminal justice system not only ignore domestic violence, but collude with those who perpetrate it. We will discuss the impact of community-based advocates losing independence as they become increasingly dependent on government-based funding. Our conclusion will show that female officers are basically left without resources. It depends on all citizens, not just those in law enforcement, to effect change.

Members of law enforcement have long referred to themselves as the "police family." They equate the love, concern and protectiveness that bonds together all those who wear the badge to the love, concern and protectiveness that bonds members of biological families. The police family, like many biological families, maintains its privacy by abiding by the absolute rule that "What happens in the family stays in the family." The loyalty, solidarity and privacy of the family must be impenetrable. This loyalty and solidarity, surrounded by a wall of privacy, protects the family from outside influence and intruders. It also leaves family members extremely vulnerable to one another. The mandate to keep what happens in the family private forbids members to reach out for anything, especially for protection against one's own.

Because of the insularity of the police culture and the unique demands of the profession, many female officers tend to date and marry male officers. These dual career couples live under a double mandate for privacy—that within their personal relationship and that within the police family. We have no way of knowing how many female officers are victims of male officers, but current domestic violence statistics estimate 30% of women in the general population will experience domestic violence; and research on police families reports the incidence to be as high as 40%. At current staffing levels, this means 23,000 to 30,000 female officers may be domestic violence victims.[3] Because of the insular nature of the culture, its masculine-identified values, and the power that the institution of policing wields, these victims have little or no protection from their abusers. To whom can an officer-victim appeal if the very institution to which she belongs colludes with her batterer?

Certain members of the male population have always used violence against women to maintain power and control within their personal relationships and, by extension, within society. Because police agencies recruit from the general population, we can reasonably assume that some of these recruits also use, condone, or will use violence against women because there is no reliable way to screen them out. However, one of the main differences between domestic violence in the general population and officer-involved domestic violence, is that the police family has managed to keep it secret for a longer time. Domestic violence in the general population has been acknowledged to be at epidemic levels for nearly 30 years. It is only in the past decade that policing has begun to acknowledge domestic violence in the ranks. This acknowledgment is far from universal as many police agencies continue to deny or ignore the problem.

The "blue wall of silence" has prevented, and continues to prevent, any honest examination of police-perpetrated domestic violence. The "powers-that-be" (PTBs) don't want the public to see how the institutional police family responds to domestic violence among their own—whether an officer is the perpetrator or the victim. They don't want the public to see the ways in which the attitudes of the police, fortified by police power, undermine society's efforts to hold batterers accountable in the criminal justice system. The institution of policing cannot afford for the public to understand the ways in which the male-dominated culture of policing fosters sexist attitudes that contribute to the psychological, sexual and physical violence that controls *all* women in our society—both civilians and officers. Ensuring that "what happens in the family stays in the family" is absolutely essential for the institution to continue preserving and protecting its own immense power.

The wall is beginning to show hairline cracks. Some police agencies are beginning to acknowledge, at least internally, that the problem exists. Some have implemented policies, protocols and officer training on police-perpetrated domestic violence since amendments to the federal gun law created new liability issues for agencies who employ convicted batterers. Some agencies are proactive; others have reacted in the aftermath of a tragic incident involving an officer.

Police-perpetrated domestic violence, like domestic violence in the general population, is so entrenched in its culture that it is foolish to think that we can simply begin where we are today and ignore its deep historical roots. Police agencies have to identify and examine the deeply ingrained beliefs, values and attitudes that have condoned and perpetuated violence against women for centuries. Acknowledging the problem, writing policy, and training officers are all steps in the right direction, yet they do not substitute for a true understanding of the issue and will not bring about substantive change.

Although it is true that not *all* men and not *all* male police officers perpetrate or condone violence against women, it is also true that *the vast majority of men do little or nothing to stop those who do*. If the majority of male officers do not condone other male officers' use of violence against women, why don't they stop them? Why don't police officials who direct the activities and priorities of law enforcement make police-perpetrated domestic violence a top priority? Why don't male police officers hold each other accountable and ostracize those officers who use violence against women just as they ostracize police officers who violate other cultural norms? Why do so many men in power accept male violence against women as if it is as natural and inevitable as the weather?

Women do not have the power to stop men's violence. Only men have that power. Males, including male police officers, frequently complain that they resent being included in the group of men who use violence against women. They accuse those of us who hold men responsible for domestic violence of reverse sexism and they are quick to point out that women are violent too. Domestic violence advocates and victims try so hard to avoid these accusations that we find ourselves not being able to speak candidly about the issue. The issue *is* male violence. If we must speak about violence against women in apolitical—mistakenly referred to as politically correct—terms, we cannot honestly speak about it at all.

Any discussion about domestic violence and males' power and control over women is bound to be volatile. This is an emotionally charged issue that involves belief systems about gender roles, social order and protection of power. The ideology of sexism and racism are embedded in the foundations of our major societal institutions, and are cornerstones of the criminal justice system. Throughout history, people have used ideology to bolster and protect power. Ideology has the advantage over logic in that it doesn't require reason or facts. It justifies its own existence. The following chapters will reveal the precarious position we find ourselves in when reason, ethics and facts do not guide the actions and decisions of those in power, but what *does* guide actions and decisions is the protection of male power.

> Violence against women is men's problem, just as racism is whites' problem, though it's women who pay the price of the one, people of color who pay the price of the other, and women of color who pay the price of both. Women can do much in our own behalf—almost everything already done to combat violence against women was done by women—but we cannot *stop* violence against women by ourselves any more than people of color can stop racism by themselves. Men *choose* to use violence to get their way. They can just as well *choose* not to. Many men choose to be non-violent, and some take a stand with women against violence and emotional abuse. They must increase their numbers, raise their voices, and use whatever power they have for change. All men *can* change their behavior. Whether they *will* is another matter.[4]

Historical, Social and Cultural Context

Each of the 16,000 police agencies and each of the 700,000 police officers in the United States have their own individual characteristics, culture and philosophy, making it difficult to generalize about agencies or officers. Sizes of departments range from one officer to tens of thousands of officers. Each agency recruits and hires officers based on variables specific to its own needs and focus. Agencies that are more law enforcement-oriented usually prefer recruits who are conservative and traditional, who believe in strict enforcement of the law and who believe in maintaining the social values and status quo of the community. Community policing-oriented agencies focus more on recruiting individuals from diverse ethnic and racial backgrounds with strong problem-solving and communication skills, and less aggressive personalities.

The police selection process serves to limit the diversity of the police. While the Commission on Accreditation for Law Enforcement Agencies (CALEA) recommends that the racial, ethnic and sexual composition of departments should reflect the composition of their communities, statistics show that few departments have achieved equity. Samuel Walker states in *The Police in America* that "racial and ethnic minority officers are underrepresented in most police departments."[5] Most fall pathetically short regarding the numbers of female and minority officers as racist and sexist barriers still remain intact. Though many major institutions lack diversity, it is particularly problematic in law enforcement because the police act as representatives of the government and as such should strive to reflect the public they serve.

Rather than choosing candidates who reflect the population of the community, many agencies choose candidates who are most likely to fit into the organization. The selection processes vary, but most tests are geared to measure "physical prowess, sexual orientation, gender identification, financial stability, employment history, and abstinence from drug and alcohol abuse."[6] Psychological evaluations and oral interviews are used to screen out those who don't conform to the middle-class status quo. "No test has been found that discriminates consistently and clearly between individuals who will and who will not make good police officers."[7]

Survival in the profession depends on an individual officer's ability to adjust to the culture by internalizing the occupational norms and values. Since white males dominate the profession of policing, those individuals who are not white and not male are forced to try to live up to white male standards and to assimilate to the white male culture. Though an individual is not white, he or she is expected to *act* white; though an individual is not male, she is expected to *act* male. Likewise, an officer may be a homosexual, but he or she should try to *act* straight. Kenji Yoshino in his book *Covering: the Hidden Assault on Our Civil Rights* explains that "to cover is to tone down a disfavored identity to fit into the mainstream. In our increasingly diverse society, all of us are outside the mainstream in some way. Nonetheless, being deemed mainstream is still often a necessity of social life." Though federal civil rights laws protect individuals against discrimination based on differences, they do "not protect individuals against demands that they mute those differences."[8]

> Policing in this country has always had the dual purpose of maintaining social order and enforcing the racial hierarchy.[9]

History is written from the perspective of those in power. Those in power have the privilege of selecting what is included or omitted from historical records. They tend to leave out historical facts that do not present them in a favorable light. The history of policing in any country reflects the history of the social values of those in power. In the United States, the history of policing reflects the struggle of white men to gain and maintain power and control over all those who are not white and not male. Several police scholars have noted that in the United States most policing texts neglect the earliest roots of policing: policing in the U.S. began during slavery.

"Colonists in Jamestown, Virginia, first purchased African slaves from Dutch traders in 1619, just a dozen years after the colony's founding. As the number of slaves grew, so did the white community's need to police them. Colonists adopted slave patrols as a formal institution by the middle of the 18th century. These were among the first police forces in the colonies. The slave codes officially established slave patrols or "paddyrollers," groups of white men charged through civic duty to keep slaves down and keep revolts from happening... Every slave-owning state had active, established patrols... They caught runaway slaves, enforced slave codes, discouraged any large gathering of blacks and generally perpetuated the atmosphere of fear that kept the slaves in line."[10] Slave owners hired other white men as patrollers to catch and return runaway slaves, authorizing them to use whatever level of force was deemed necessary to capture and return a rebellious slave. If the slave resisted, the patroller was authorized to kill the slave. Social rights scholars note that this was the beginning of the criminalization of blacks in U.S. society, making runaway slaves the first large group of criminals in the United States.[11]

It wasn't until the 1940s, when racial tensions increased, that police agencies began to hire black males to police black communities. Many white officers and citizens were outraged that law enforcement agencies would hire those who historically were *policed* to do the policing. In their view, granting police power and authority to blacks turned reality and social order upside-down. Many white officers deeply resented that police agencies were inviting black men to enter *their* profession.

In an effort to quell their resentment and fear, agencies granted the black officers only limited police powers, segregated them from white officers, and restricted them to beats in black neighborhoods with only the worst cars and equipment. White officers hazed them, refused to speak to them, isolated them in segregated facilities, and some even segregated black officers during training exercises. In some cities, black officers were denied the right to carry arms, they were not issued uniforms and their badge numbers distinguished them from whites. In the 1950s, black officers were watched "to ensure that they did not commit the most serious offense that a black officer could commit in the South: arresting a white citizen."[12] "Throughout the 1960s black police officers continued to work on "black beats," to supervise only other black officers, and to be excluded from elite squads and divisions in the police departments… Merit promotions also eluded them."[13]

As the national Civil Rights Movement gained momentum, "black officers began to file suits to win promotions, back pay, and equality as police officers."[14] However, they still were treated primarily as tokens and remained excluded from command positions. They were enlisted in the "wars" against drugs, gangs and violence in the black community. Their continuing mandate was to control the black population and serve as buffers and liaisons between "their" people and the rest of the (white) population. The only way black officers could do the job was to "support, endorse, endure and recognize a race-based system where the position of black police officers was inherently inferior to that of white police officers. Black officers were restricted to quasi-officer status, official impotence, and mandated inaction on their part with respect to violations by white offenders."[15]

The flood of immigrants into America's cities in the 1800s brought new ethnic groups to be policed. Simultaneously, there was a dramatic shift occuring in the role of women that threatened the status quo. Women began seeking independence, working outside the home at brutal jobs for long hours and low wages. Their only outlets for pleasure were "dangerous dance-halls" where women encountered the "snares and pitfalls that could

> "Fallen women" and "wayward girls" became new categories of description. Delinquents of all kinds were overwhelmingly female because, as Vida Hunt Francis asked, "Who has ever heard of a fallen boy?"[17]

befall innocent women—sullied environments and brutal men."[16]

Social workers became obsessed with "looking after" these women and girls who had no male protection—runaway children, prostitutes, unwed mothers, and women escaping violent husbands—and treated them as objects of investigation, classification, and documentation. Social workers were primarily middle-class white women, and while they did not enjoy the professional status of male psychiatrists, physicians and police, their values still reflected class power, privilege and "notions of racial superiority." They "targeted impoverished, immigrant, and working-class clients"[18] without the means to live up to middle class standards, but whose low social status was attributed to underlying moral qualities rather than to the "inequities of gender, class, race and ethnicity."[19]

Society saw the profession of policing as one of fighting crime and protecting men's property, not administering to the needs of wayward or abused women and children. But there were clearly a lot of women and children who needed protection from the violence and neglect of men, so police departments began to hire women to tend to them. They recruited women with backgrounds in social work because they thought women would be able to relate to, understand and communicate with other females who only had "women's problems."

Shortly after World War I, women were allowed to perform "protective patrol work":

> The woman patrol officer will concern herself with any situation arising in a place open to the public which might be considered as potentially harmful to women and

children. She will give attention to downtown streets, depots, docks, parks, public restrooms, burlesque theaters, moving picture houses, amusement parks, tourists camps, employment agencies for unskilled and semi-skilled workers, questionable hotels, rooming houses, dance halls, cabarets, barbecues, suspected beer-flats, suspected blind-pigs and suspected disorderly houses. She will look for truants from home and school, unemployed girls, men looking for pick-ups, girls soliciting for prostitution, drug peddlers, procurers, other underworld characters, obscene posters and salacious literature. The officers are also looking for intoxicated girls, children engaged in street trades, and disorderly conduct in parked cars.[20]

The majority of male officers were astonished that law enforcement agencies would hire those who historically were the *protected* sex to *do* the protecting. In their view, granting police power and authority to women turned reality and social order upside-down. Many male officers deeply resented that police agencies were inviting females to enter *their* profession. The institution of policing retained male police officers' monopoly on power, however, by granting female officers only very limited police authority. Agencies denied female officers authority to arrest men, and often did not issue them weapons. In addition, departments held them to strict standards of femininity in their uniforms, "ladylike" behavior and segregated training. Many agencies created Women's Bureaus which further segregated the female officers. "They were restricted to a separate job category of police*woman*, excluded from

> November 1968: Indianapolis (IN) police officers Elizabeth Robinson and Betty Blakenship are assigned control of Car 47. They are the first women in the United States assigned to a patrol car.[21]

many assignments, including patrol, and in some departments not eligible for promotions above a certain rank."[22] As they were in no way equal to male officers, they posed no real threat to males in the profession; they were at best "helpers" and at worst, an inconvenience.

The Civil Rights Act of 1964 made it illegal to discriminate on the basis of sex, race, color, religion and national origin. Gender, however, was originally included in the bill with the intention of *preventing* its passage. The following is one of those interesting historical facts that is commonly left out of our mainstream history books: the Civil Rights Act was never intended to grant women employment rights under Title VII. Southerners were opposed to the bill and wanted to kill it at all costs, so they included gender as a category. "Reasoning that the *addition of protections for women would be seen as both silly and radical*, [Rep. Howard Smith (VA)] figured he had provided colleagues with the perfect excuse for voting against the bill without seeming racist. Ultimately the joke was on Smith, because the bill passed."[23]

Female officers' status as "social workers in uniforms" began to change after the passage of the 1972 Equal Employment Opportunity Act (EEOA) and the subsequent consent decrees that forced departments to comply with the law. The National Center for Women and Policing (NCWP) documented that "the biggest gains for women in sworn law enforcement are often seen in agencies that are subject to a consent decree or other court order that mandates the hiring and/or promotion of qualified women."[24] They were granted patrol assignments, enlisted in the vice squad, and even "allowed" to patrol without males riding along. It surprised many when the Police Foundation conducted a study and found that "women officers carried out their duties effectively. The only variance from the performance of male officers was that they made fewer arrests and gave fewer traffic citations. The studies also found that women police officers were less likely than their male counterparts to engage in unbecoming conduct."[25]

Of concern today is that the consent decrees that were put into place in the 1970s and 1980s are expiring. "Unfortunately, there is evidence to suggest that progress in these agencies often erodes as soon as the consent decree expires or is otherwise lifted by the courts… Without consent decrees imposed to remedy discriminatory hiring and employment practices by law enforcement agencies, it is clear that the marginal gains women have made in policing would not have been possible."[26] The NCWP also states that at the present rate of increase, it will take generations for women to be proportionately represented in police agencies. In May 2006, the U.S. DOJ Bureau of Justice Statistics released their report on local law enforcement agencies. There are approximately 77,250 full-time sworn female officers serving in municipal, sheriff and state agencies—11% of all full-time sworn officers. Women of color account for 4%. As might be expected, female officers fare better in larger cities, but such agencies account for only 2% of departments. Nearly half of local law enforcement agencies in the United States employ fewer than 10 officers.[27] (Table 1)

Table 1
Local Police Departments, 2003 Demographics

Full-time Sworn Officers (N=683,599)

Ethnicity	Total	Male	Female
Total	100%	88.7%	11.3%
Caucasian	76.4	76.4	7.0
African-American	11.7	11.7	2.7
Hispanic	9.0	9.1	1.3
Others	2.8	2.8	0.3

Agency Size (N=15,766)

Size	Agencies	Full-time sworn officers
1000 or greater	0.4%	34.1%
500–999	0.3	6.1
250–499	0.8	8.0
100–249	3.2	12.8
50–99	6.7	12.5
25–49	13.1	11.8
10–24	30.0	10.2
1–94	5.5	4.5

Population Served

Population	Agencies	Full-time sworn officers
1 million or greater	0.1%	21.6%
500,000–999,999	0.3	11.0
250,000–499,999	0.3	7.1
100,000–249,999	1.4	11.1
50,000–99,999	3.3	11.1
25,000–49,999	6.1	10.8
10,000–24,999	14.9	13.0
2500–9999	32.0	10.0
Under 2500	41.5	4.0

Source: *Local Police Departments, 2003.*
Bureau of Justice Statistics (2006)[28]

The EEOA, under which departments could no longer discriminate by denying women and minorities full police powers and authority, posed a serious threat to white males' monopoly on power within the institution of policing. A swell of protests came from white males claiming that "others" were taking law enforcement positions that rightfully belonged to them. There was much more to this protest than mere employment—it was about who in America will be in charge of whom, who will have power over whom, and who will enforce the social norms and the laws. It was and still is about race and gender and the preservation and protection of white male power.

Despite the EEOA and new hiring policies, those at the top of the institutional hierarchy were able to ensure that the white male hierarchy remained intact. Today, white males still retain the vast majority of the decision-making and policy-making positions in law enforcement. When white men make the policy decisions from their perspective, this profoundly influences the way members of all minority groups experience their work as officers on a daily basis. It also profoundly influences the way that police work is done and the way the public perceives the police.

Many individual police officers in the dominant group claim that they personally don't feel all that powerful and certainly do not see themselves as oppressors. Martha Burk, in *The Cult of Power*, notes that "most enlightened men would say that they don't believe males are superior, and at a rational level, they would be telling the truth. But at the gut level—what psychologists call *cultural conditioning*—men have been indoctrinated with the opposite view."[30] The oppression of women in policing depends on the average, ordinary male officer to maintain it, and many of them deeply resent what they perceive to be the invasion of their turf. They fear they are losing legitimacy and power, and believe it is imperative to stop this poaching. Moreover, they think women receive special treatment and consideration, and the white men see themselves as victims of reverse discrimination.

> It's not that abusive men think of themselves as soldiers in the cause of male supremacy; their demands and disappointments are individual, specific complaints which they can enunciate, and do, often in very loud voices... Men who beat their wives were not ideologues defending the dominance of their sex... They were using violence to increase their control over particular women, defending real, material benefits. Dinner on the table, cold beer on call, sex on demand, quiet kids, clean socks—all those benefits to which a man "naturally" feels entitled... Their sense of entitlement was so strong it was experienced as a need.[29]

Though racism and sexism are both strong in policing, sexism proves to be even stronger. Male officers of all racial backgrounds bond and unite on one thing—their resistance to hiring and promoting females. Even men who do not occupy positions of power at the top echelons of the hierarchy derive a sense of entitlement and superiority simply because they are men. The lowest heterosexual man in the hierarchy enjoys a sense of superiority over even the highest-ranked woman. Black male officers, though discriminated against on the basis of race, gain more from being male than they lose from being black. Many police officers, both black and white, acknowledge that black male officers have more status in the organization than does any female officer.

> *Black females on the job get a lot of flak from the black officers. You would expect them to be supportive of us... after what* they *had to endure. And then we come on—when females came on, white, black, whatever... the attitude was "We're not the ones being picked on anymore. The guys that came on in the sixties and seventies—those are black males and they have an attitude toward black females. It's just* there. *They don't accept us on the job. They take it as you're taking their job. You're taking a man's job.*[31]

> *I have this white female lieutenant; her and I used to butt heads together. And I... used to complain about some of the stuff that they did. And because we didn't talk, we didn't know what was going on, so she told me one day... "Oh, that happened to me, too." I say, "You're kidding... You mean to tell me all this time I thought they were doing this to me because I was black." "Oh, no, I could have told you they're doing it because we're women."*[32]

> *I came to the realization that I am black before I am blue. I realized that I, as a black person, was only tolerated but not accepted. I was black because that is the title that society has given me, and I am referred to as blue when I wear my police uniform. On the numerous times that I have seen fellow white officers, men and women, in an off duty capacity... [they] did not care to know who I am, but they were more concerned about what I am, I am Black.*[33]

The following quote from Feagin & Vera's *White Racism: The Basics* well-illustrates the parallels between racism and sexism. Note how readily one can substitute the word "sexism" for "racism."

"Racism is more than a matter of individual prejudice and scattered episodes of discrimination. There is no black racism because there is no centuries-old system of racialized subordination and discrimination designed by African Americans to exclude white Americans from full participation in the rights, privileges, and benefits of this society. Black (or other minority) racism would require not only a widely accepted racist ideology directed at whites but also the power to systematically exclude whites from opportunities and rewards in major economic, cultural, and political institutions. While there are black Americans with antiwhite prejudices, and there are instances of blacks discriminating against whites, these… are not part of an entrenched structure of institutionalized racism that can be found in every nook and cranny of this country."[34]	Sexism is more than a matter of individual prejudice and scattered episodes of discrimination. There is no female sexism because there is no centuries-old system of sexualized subordination and discrimination designed by women to exclude American men from full participation in the rights, privileges, and benefits of this society. Female sexism would require not only a widely accepted sexist ideology directed at men but also the power to systematically exclude men from opportunities and rewards in major economic, cultural, and political institutions. While there are American women with anti-male prejudices, and there are instances of women discriminating against men, these… are not part of an entrenched structure of institutionalized sexism that can be found in every nook and cranny of this country.

Black officers may be ambivalent about acting as agents of social control over blacks and perpetuating the injustices of the white-dominated criminal justice system. These officers have to accept the racial status quo and live the paradox of being a black police officer in a society that not only denies power to blacks, but also criminalizes *being* black. If they choose to survive in policing, however, they are forced to participate in, and therefore perpetuate, the racist bias of the system. In order to survive, some black officers have adopted the same attitudes held by white officers. Straddling the divide between two cultures, they have been accused of being sell-outs within the black community and of being soft on their "brothers" within the police community.

Similar to black male officers, females have had to choose their best survival technique. Many female officers describe their ambivalence about acting as agents of social control over women, and having to enforce the laws of the male-dominated criminal justice system. Female police officers have to accept the gender-based status quo and live the paradox of being a female police officer in a society that denies authority to women. Female officers are required to enforce laws that they know are discriminatory. If they choose to survive in policing, however, they are required to participate in the sexist bias of the system.

Since the passage of the Civil Rights Act, many traditional and conservative white men in the general population have been alarmed that the social order is crumbling. Not only are women and minorities making some progress in society and in the workplace, laws against wife-beating and marital rape threaten male dominance and control—even within the sanctity of a man's home. In the aftermath of the Civil Rights and Women's Movements, many officers felt betrayed and confused: the rules had changed in the middle of the game. The PTBs were now ordering them to protect the "rights" of minorities and women... what happened to *their* rights?

Reactive Policies

Many departments assign female officers primarily to work with violent crimes against women, the majority of which are assault and battery and sexual assault perpetrated by women's intimate partners. Men are committing these violent crimes against women at epidemic proportions because of the fundamental belief systems that support and justify male dominance in intimate relationships. The man is entitled to be the head of the household, and all other family members are subordinate to him. Along with his material property, a man's wife and children reflect on his worth and status and serve as symbols of his power. For centuries, our laws denied women the right to vote, own property or retain custody of their children. The spirit of these laws protected men who used coercion and violence to control and dominate women and children.

> By the beginning of the twentieth century, an American mother enjoyed the right to custody only in nine states and in the District of Columbia; and only if a state judge found her morally and economically worthy of motherhood.[35]

Police officers have historically resisted getting involved in "domestic disputes" because they were uncomfortable interfering with a male's entitlement to do as he pleases in his own home. Having been socialized to see violence against women as a woman's just dessert for getting out of line, many police officers considered a husband's or lover's violence against a woman to be *her* problem. The police defended their lack of intervention by arguing that society employed police to protect the safety of the general population, not to protect every individual woman who chose to defy her man's authority. It was a *privilege*, not a right, for a woman to be free of violence.

Many women, however, saw it differently. In the spirit of the Civil Rights Movement of the 1970s, women voiced their conviction that it was the job of the government and the police to provide equal protection of the law to the millions of women who were being beaten and raped by intimate partners and male household members. Women succeeded in getting the government to pass legislation criminalizing domestic violence in most states. This resulted in the obligation of police officers to enforce the laws. Still, many police departments continued to give domestic violence calls low priority until 1983 when Tracey Thurman sued the city of Torrington, CT for violation of her 14th Amendment guarantee of equal protection. In this landmark case, the federal court awarded her $2.3 million in compensatory damages. Police agency liability became a strong motivating force for crafting domestic violence policies and protocols.[36]

> Thurman v. City of Torrington (1984): The suit charged that the Torrington Police Department condoned a pattern or practice of affording inadequate protection, or no protection at all, to women who have complained of having been abused by their husbands or others with whom they have had close relations… The final incident took place June 10, 1983 when Charles Thurman stabbed Tracey Thurman in the chest, neck and throat with a knife 10 minutes after she had called police. One police officer arrived at the scene 25 minutes after the call was made,

and that officer did nothing to stop Charles Thurman from kicking his estranged wife in the head... Thurman was arrested only after several other police officers arrived at the scene and Thurman... again made a threatening move toward his wife.[37]

The adoption of policy brought about the need to train officers how to respond to domestic disputes. The quality and the quantity of the training still varies by department. Many police instructors believe that it is too daunting a task to change individual officers' sexist beliefs and attitudes, their only goal is to ensure that an officer's *actions* are in accordance with department policy and protocol. Anthony Bouza disagrees with this approach to domestic violence training:

> In domestic violence cases, training is not only needed to teach the cops how to deal with this challenge, but perhaps even more important, to change their prevailing attitudes as well. Training is usually geared toward improving operational techniques. Training is normally content to leave the attitudes alone, and, usually, that's a wise decision. Attitudes usually take too long to change. It's a lot easier to change behavior than thought. But this is a case where attitudes drive actions and, unless the one is changed, the performance will be pro forma and fail, making domestic abuse one of the few areas where the training must strongly emphasize the need for the proper philosophical approach.[38]

When a department fails to address their officers' sexist beliefs and attitudes regarding male violence against women, male officers (and female officers who are male-identified) are likely to bring the traditional, conservative male perspective and approach to the problem—if a man hits a woman she probably deserves it or provoked it. These officers may also believe that the woman is prone to lie about or exaggerate what actually took place, resulting in their giving more credibility to the alleged perpetrator's side of the story.

Research shows that most female officers respond to domestic violence calls more effectively than their male colleagues do. They bring a woman's perspective and experience to the scene. They understand how men use violence to maintain the imbalance of power in intimate relationships. They may understand the innuendo of the abuser's threats to the victim more than a male officer would. They may see the significance of certain types of evidence that a male officer might miss, like torn wedding photographs and other types of symbolic violence. Female officers (who are not male-identified) tend to define the situation, interview the witness, write their reports, and give different testimony than male officers. Women officers are able to see the incident through the eyes of the victim instead of through the eyes of the perpetrator.

Female officers who have not become male-identified bring a woman's perspective, intuition, insight and life experience to the job. Today, an estimated 50% of calls for police service are for domestics and sexual assaults. Female officers who see through the female gender lens are more empathetic and sympathetic to victims of domestic violence and sexual assault; they believe what female victims tell them. Female officers may judge rapists and male perpetrators of domestic violence quite differently than male officers do. These officers have the potential to overthrow the social order by challenging the gender imbalance of power. They pose a serious threat to men's monopoly of power in society and in policing. These women are working toward the redefinition of policing. They are challenging the PTBs in a struggle over who gets to decide what policing is about: toughness, physical violence and power to enforce the law, or communication, understanding people, solving problems and keeping the peace in a community.

> Joseph Wambaugh... recommended a woman police chief and a police force of 50% women or more because "female cops can go a long way toward helping to mitigate the super-aggressive, paramilitary macho myth of the gung-ho cop and introducing the sobering element of maturity in police work." Women, he said, can reveal and discuss their emotions in a way that men, especially young men, cannot. By acknowledging the fear that accompanies physical danger, women police officers accept it without shame or bravado. Because "they don't need to whip on somebody because he scared them" and are more willing "to back off and wait for help" instead of saving face by busting heads, they can set an example of calm, considered, and compassionate response that men can learn, however slowly, to follow. Police work... is not about physical altercations... [or] about shooting people... It's about talking to people and problem solving, tasks for which women are "eminently better qualified than men."[39]

The Police Culture

If you want to play in a man's world, you have to play by their rules.

Police training is designed to transform the recruit's civilian identity into that of a police officer. A recruit learns that the police culture values group allegiance and solidarity, conformity to established standards and norms, unquestioning obedience to superior officers, and respect for rank and authority. They learn to be submissive to superiors but intolerant toward those who do not submit to their own authority. They become loyal to the values of their own group, willing to do what they are told, and show an extremely hostile attitude toward people who are different than themselves.[40] The recruit becomes a member of an exclusive fraternity that wields the power of law enforcement.

> *Women are treated throughout their career the way recruits are treated through their probationary period. The hazing and lack of "full membership" stops for a male recruit once they have proven themselves yet continues on for women.*
>
> *I recall being told to "sit there, don't touch anything, and we'll get along fine" by my first training officer as I entered his patrol car for the first time. I realized it was going to be a long eight hours, and an even longer one-month assignment.*

Though male and female recruits go through the same training and indoctrination into police culture, the effects and impact are quite different. Men and women come into the training and culture with different backgrounds and socialization. It is easy for men to fit into the culture because they are already socialized in the male-dominated and male-oriented hierarchy of power. They have been socialized and conditioned since childhood to see the world in terms of male power networks and survival of the fittest. Valued male qualities include strength, competitiveness, aggression, logic, self-confidence, dominance and emotional control. Women however, have been socialized and conditioned to see the world in terms of social relationships and peacekeeping. Valued female qualities include beauty, cooperativeness, compassion, intuition, indecisiveness, dependence and emotionality.

> When women look out on the world they see themselves reflected as women in a few narrow areas of life such as "caring" occupations (teaching, nursing, child care) and personal relationships. To see herself as a leader, for example, a woman must first get around the fact that leadership itself has been gendered through its identification with maleness and masculinity as part of… culture. While a man might have to learn to see himself as a manager, a woman has to be able to see herself as a *woman* manager who can succeed in spite of the fact that she isn't a man. As a result, any woman who dares to strive for standing in the world beyond the sphere of caring relationships must choose between two very different cultural images of who she is and ought to be. For her to assume real public power… she must resolve a contradiction between her culturally based identity as a woman, on the one hand, and the male-identified *position* that she occupies on the other. For this reason, the more powerful a woman is [in this culture], the more "unsexed"

she becomes in the eyes of others as her female cultural identity recedes beneath the mantle of male-identified power and masculine images associated with it. With men the effect is just the opposite: the more powerful they are, the more aware we are of their maleness. Power looks sexy on men but not on women.[41]

Historically, entering the military or policing has been the epitome of masculinity. In many respects, the two careers still remain males' last bastions. The hyper-masculine culture of policing glorifies masculinity as much as it abhors the presence of anything feminine in the culture. The bottom line is that "policing is a man's job and a man's world" and women have no legitimate place in it. Its traditional and conservative ideology affirms the polarization of gender roles. In this worldview, a female officer is an oxymoron.

> *During Academy, we had to box and wrestle men, for street fight conditioning. I was fighting in the gym environment with a male peer. He was in the process of choking me out; I could feel that I was starting to go out so I grabbed his testicles. The instructor stopped the fight and said, "Oh no, honey, you aren't allowed to do that." He was willing to let the male officer choke me out but I couldn't squeeze his testicles to get him to stop and get off of me!*

> *During a self-defense class, I was supposed to throw this guy who was highly trained in one of the martial arts. I had trained in college and earned a brown belt in jujitsu, so I felt confident. He grabbed me from behind—but as I turned to throw him, he grabbed my sweatshirt and pulled it up over my head. I stood there in my bra, totally embarrassed, while the class laughed and laughed.*[42]

Men's arguments against women in policing are many. Some believe that women aren't physically strong enough or emotionally tough enough to do the job. Some believe the job is too dangerous for a woman and that female officers make the job more dangerous because they aren't capable of providing back-up or effectively fighting. Some believe the presence of female officers distracts the male officers because they feel the need to protect the women, or because they are sexually attracted to them. Most feel that the presence of women interferes with male bonding and jeopardizes male solidarity.

Many men in policing believe, as do many men in other professions, that the inclusion of women threatens the status, prestige and mystique of the formerly exclusively male profession. Yet, studies consistently show that women are as good or better police officers than men. Women are better at de-escalating potentially violent confrontations. They often have better communication skills and are able to gain citizens' cooperation and trust without resorting to excessive force. And they more effectively respond to crimes of violence against women.

> Three decades of research on women in policing are indisputable: women use a style of policing that relies more on communication and less on the use of force. Female police have dramatically fewer excessive-use-of-force and other misconduct complaints than their male counterparts do. Female police excel in de-escalating violent and volatile situations, in carrying out community policing goals, and in fostering the cooperation and trust of the community. They treat violence against women and children more seriously, crimes which account for more than a third of all police calls. At the same time, the research shows that female officers are as fully capable and willing as male officers to use force when necessary. Fully integrating women into law enforcement is the essential and best

remedy for improving policing, and for fixing the flaws that have plagued law enforcement for decades.[43]

These facts don't matter. Many remain loyal to the stereotypes, myths and male bias because male power is at stake. Men view women's strengths as weaknesses and women's assets as liabilities. It doesn't matter what the research shows when confronting an ideology or prejudice. White men in power define what policing is. They define the ideal characteristics and attributes of officers. They define what makes a "good cop"—and a good cop is a male cop.

> *Without exception, never in my career have I had a male colleague stand up to and challenge another male colleague who was denigrating women police. They keep silent. They might tell you in private that women police are good at their jobs, but not in the presence of "the culture."*[44]

Some people question why women want to join such a male-dominated, male-oriented institution as law enforcement. Women provide a variety of answers to that question. Some women, like their male counterparts, are attracted to policing because they seek to wield the power the job confers. Many say that they chose the profession for the same reasons men chose it. They want to help people and make a difference in society. They want to have meaningful,

> Pia Kinney James, recently retired Madison PD Investigator recalled the tense, often silent hours in her training officer's patrol car: "You took some man's job. How's he supposed to support his family?" she recalled him saying. Then a divorced mother, [she] said, "How am I supposed to support my family?"[45]

steady employment that compensates them with a decent salary, benefits and pension.

Some female officers who intend to advance in their careers believe that advancement depends on individual ability and skill. Some are resigned to the fact that "it's a man's world" and are satisfied to get whatever piece of the pie they can, considering themselves fortunate to have any of it at all. Some are willing to play by the boys' rules to get where they want to go, and are willing to compromise their personal values and femininity in order to do it.

Others identify systemic barriers that prevent women from advancing and they aspire to remove those barriers. These are the women who are trail-blazers; they seek to improve the status of women in policing in the future. They don't want to assimilate into the male-dominated culture, they want to change it. They see women who are trying to be "one of the boys" as detrimental to all women in policing, and want instead to gain recognition and appreciation for the attributes women bring to policing. Many want to change the focus of policing, making law enforcement more about social justice than social control.

> Painted in giant lettering on the academy gym wall: "Always cheat, always win."

All social institutions have formal and informal cultures. The formal culture consists of rules and regulations, policies and procedures. For example, city and police administrators decide the formal police culture—they write the rules and regulations, policies and procedures of the agency. These formal documents usually address the focus of the agency, detail procedures to ensure the protection of citizens and property, and include disciplinary guidelines. They also serve to protect the police agency from liability.

The informal culture—its "ethos"—consists of the day-to-day customs and practices within the institution. These are the actual work habits of the employees and the reality of the way they function in their jobs. In policing, recruits learn the formal culture in the academy. They learn the informal culture during field training where they not only learn how to survive on the streets but also how to survive in the agency.

> *Forget what you learned in the Academy... this is the real world.*

Every police officer at every level of responsibility knows that discrepancies exist between the formal and informal culture. Each must choose when and whether to ignore, trivialize or deny these discrepancies. In many instances, ignoring their existence is a requirement for survival on the job. "The first female officers performed their duties in an atmosphere of disbelief on the part of their supervisors and peers in their ability to deal physically and emotionally with the rigors of street work, particularly patrol functions. It must be remembered that peer acceptance is one of the greatest pressures operating within the police organization. The desire to be identified as a "good officer" is a strong motivating force, and a failure to achieve that goal in one's eyes and in the eyes of one's peers can have a devastating and demoralizing effect."[46]

> *I think you are forced to adapt to cultural norms. If you don't, you're ostracized and that will affect your safety. Some officers may not rush to your aid quite as quickly as they should. I've seen women leave because of this. You have to walk a fine line all of the time.*

The ethos of bravery does not allow officers to admit to fear, pain or any emotion. It dictates that officers are never to back down from a fight or run from danger. The ethos dictates that officers must go to any extreme to gain control and to do whatever they have to do to maintain it. Officers must appear to be confident and competent at all times. They must rely on their training, not their human instincts, when entering a dangerous environment. They have to hide their fear, lock down their emotions, put on their game face—and take control of the situation no matter what. They may be scared or in pain, but they have to *act* as if they are not.

Men are not accustomed to living in fear, while women are. Whether she is a civilian or an officer, a woman lives with the constant awareness that she may be randomly targeted by a man simply because she is a woman.

> Look closely at her.
>
> She crosses a city street, juggling her briefcase and her sack of groceries. Or she walks down a dirt road... Or she hurries toward her locked car, pulling a small child with her...
>
> Suddenly there are footsteps behind her. Heavy, rapid. A man's footsteps. She knows this immediately, just as she knows that she must not look around. She quickens her pace in time to the quickening of her pulse. She is afraid. He could be a rapist... a robber, a killer. He could be none of these. He could be a man merely walking at his normal pace. But she fears him. She fears him because he is a man. She has reason to fear.
>
> She does not feel the same way... if she hears a woman's footsteps behind her. It is the footstep of a man she fears. This moment she shares with every human being who is female.[47]

Women have learned to handle their fear. While social conditioning allows them to express emotions, such expression makes men uncomfortable, so women end up hiding their true feelings. They have learned to present the appearance of well-being even when they are feeling pain or fear: they have become proficient actors. This ability to hide emotions, however, is a survival technique rather than an attempt to gain and maintain control of others. Men often misinterpret this as women being manipulative. (While men, too, are acting when they hide or disguise their emotions, it is seen as a sign of strength rather than weakness or manipulation.) A woman's survival frequently requires her to de-escalate a situation and avoid confrontation. She has learned that assertiveness, rather than aggression, often works best. Men, however, are socialized to fight, to deny fear or intimidation and to not be controlled by emotions. In order to suppress their pain and/or fear, they often act violently and aggressively when facing a threat.

The female officer faces a Catch-22 in the police culture: she can deny or suppress her emotions, be aggressive and fight to demonstrate that she is a competent officer because she can "act like a man," or she can avoid using threats or violence, and be criticized for "acting like a woman." Under the ethos of bravery, she must choose. She cannot act as both an officer and a woman.

> *It didn't mean it was any easier for me and it certainly meant that, you know, I might go home and bawl my eyes out, but you never let the bastards see you cry.*
>
> *Sheriff Margo Frasier (Travis County, TX): "When women first came into policing, the concern was that we weren't strong enough, we weren't tough... We've been learning our whole lives how to deal with things without having to resort to physical strength and physical violence. I think*

> *the thing we most bring in is the ability to handle situations without having to ever lay hands on."*[48]

The ethos of autonomy justifies officers scoffing at formal policies and refusing to go by the book. They consider policies and protocols the product of ivory tower thinking by administrators who have no idea what it takes to survive on the street. And, because no policy can exhaustively cover the wide range of situations that patrol officers encounter on the job, agencies grant police the power of discretion. Patrol officers place a high value on their power of discretion because it allows them to "define the situation," meaning they can call it as they see it, and take whatever action they deem appropriate under the circumstances. Patrol officers, though low in rank, have this power and use it under little, if any, supervision on the street.

Again, as with the ethos of bravery, the power of discretion, when used with valid judgment, is a valuable tool in effective law enforcement. It is unreasonable and potentially dangerous to require patrol officers to check with command before taking certain actions. But it is also reasonable and potentially safer to require the same officers to follow established policies and procedures.

The different worldviews of male and female officers may cause them to perceive and define the same situation quite differently. Men are socialized to believe that their perception of reality *is* reality. This instills a confidence that allows them to take swift and sure action based on their personal judgment of a situation. Women, however, are socialized to deliberate, seek others' input, and to evaluate their own perception of reality. In the male-defined culture of policing, many male officers believe female officers' thoughtful deliberation indicates that they are incapable of independent thought, accurate perception of reality, or swift and sure action. And, when a female officer's perception of reality differs from that of a male's, her perception is commonly considered to be the inaccurate one.

The exercise of discretionary power can lead to inconsistent and discriminatory policing. The decision whether or not to enforce the law in a particular situation may be laden with social and political implications and consequences. While a female or minority officer may accuse a white male officer of sexist or racist judgment, a white male officer may accuse a female officer of reverse sexism because he sees her as being biased in favor of a female citizen, or accuse a black officer of reverse racism for being biased in favor of a black man. White male police officers may be threatened by what they perceive to be reverse sexism and racism because it jeopardizes their monopoly on the power to define reality, a basic source of white men's power.

Male officers trust each other to abide by the code of silence, but many fear that women will not. They know the guys will stick together and not contradict each other. They know that even when their version of the story is not truthful, they will not be caught because the golden rule says, "What happens here stays here." Everyone understands the dire consequences of violating the code.

Many men will go along to get along and not contradict or challenge other officers' behaviors or actions. They have been socialized to be part of the team and to cover one another's "indiscretions" because that's what being a team member means. Women officers, too, learn to value team solidarity. However, they usually are not as strongly socialized as men are to be loyal to the group at the expense of their individual beliefs. They often experience intense ambivalence about abiding by the code, especially in the face of harassment, discrimination and brutality.

Many male officers devalue the feminine perspective, qualities and skills precisely because they dismantle the mystique of the macho cop. They feel threatened that women's assets may make the male's physical strength and emotional toughness obsolete as qualifications for the job. In *Understanding Police Culture*, Crank states, "Police organizations historically have been male in spirit and gender."[50] Though some say this has changed, Crank observes that "at a cultural level, little has changed since Martin published her seminal work in 1980. In spite of increasing recruitment of women into traditional male police assignments, masculinity continues to be a powerful theme of police culture… Today department policies do not permit gender abuse. This has shifted the location of bias, but has not fundamentally changed it."[51]

> Male patrol officers, denying the existence of gender discrimination in a progressive midwestern police department, told researchers that when anyone joins the force, "We just want to know if you are a team player, if you keep your mouth shut, if you don't tattle to the brass, and if you can be counted on for backup." Even assuming that the men intended to include basic competence in their evaluation, it seems remarkable that three of four stated grounds for inclusion and acceptance of women refer to assimilation into the existing culture rather than to performance on the job, and two of four relate to the often denied but often demonstrated code of silence.[49]

Postulates of Secrecy & Solidarity

Don't give up another cop.
Watch out for your partner first and then the rest of the guys working that tour.
If you get caught off base, don't implicate anybody else.
Make sure the other guys know if another cop is dangerous or "crazy."
Don't get involved in anything in another cop's sector.
Hold up your end of the work; don't leave work for the next tour.
Don't look for favors just for yourself.

Postulates of Isolation

Protect your ass.
Don't trust a new guy until you have him checked out.
Don't talk too little or too much; don't tell anybody more than they have to know.
Don't trust bosses to look out for your interests.

Postulates of Bravery

Show balls.
Be aggressive when you have to, but don't be too eager.[52]

> Racism and other forms of bigotry are often disclosed in the feel of a place. An institution may have an atmosphere of insidious bigotry that could never be proved in litigation.[53]

Though legally required to hire women and minorities, there are many ways to circumvent the spirit of the law. The covert and subtle ways that men discriminate against women in organizations, including policing, combine and result in systemic barriers. Marilyn Frye compares systemic barriers to a birdcage: "If you look very closely at just one wire in the cage, you cannot see the other wires. [You are] unable to see why a bird would not just fly around the single wire any time it wanted. Furthermore, even if you… inspected each wire, you still could not see why a bird would have trouble going past the wires to get anywhere. There is no physical property of any one wire, nothing that the closest scrutiny could discover, that will reveal how a bird could be inhibited or harmed by it except in the most accidental way. It is only when you step back, stop looking at the wires one by one… and see the whole cage, that you can see why the bird does not go anywhere, and then you will see it in a moment. The bird is surrounded by a network of systematically related barriers, no one of which would be the least hindrance to its flight, but which, by their relations to each other, are as confining as the solid walls of a dungeon."[54]

In order to remain in the profession, women and minorities have had to tolerate a hostile work environment of both overt and subtle harassment and discrimination. Police agencies usually deny that there are systemic barriers for women or minorities. They claim that management does not discriminate in training opportunities or promotions. Some agencies have learned through costly discrimination lawsuits that they cannot afford to be overtly discriminatory, so they employ covert and subtle ways to perpetuate the male hierarchy.

> *Every time I applied for a sergeant's position I was knocked back, questions were asked like, "How do you think the men would respond to a woman in charge?"*

Female officers report that male officers and supervisors closely monitor and scrutinize their behavior and decisions. Knowing they are being watched, they become even more self-conscious and nervous, which causes them to make mistakes. Men then exaggerate those mistakes and use them as proof that females are incompetent to do the job, generalizing the mistakes to all women officers. This often has the effect of making the women monitor and judge their own behavior from a male perspective, causing them to adjust their behavior to fit the masculine standard.

Though discriminatory or harassing behavior is officially against the rules, many supervisors covertly give men the message that they can do and say whatever they want against women as long as they don't get caught. When male superiors address female peers or subordinates with the term "honey" or "sweetheart" they reinforce this message. Some male officers admit that when women aren't around they use derogatory language, talking about women as pieces of ass, tits and cunts. The men ridicule and tell stories about female officers to damage their reputations and/or undermine their authority. If the men are caught, they deny it. If a female officer hears and confronts them, they accuse her of being paranoid, exaggerating, mishearing, "reading into it," or being out to get them. If she reports the incident, the department might be forced to acknowledge it took place, but then employ the "isolated incident" defense and deny that it is actually habitual and customary practice.

Some supervisors and instructors get away with insults and slurs by saying they are part of training and that they are trying to "toughen up" the officers and prepare them for what they will experience on the street. If a woman reacts or reports the behavior, the instructor will say that he didn't mean anything by it and that she isn't calloused enough to handle the job. In 2003, after a female Deputy identified a male Training Officer who had engaged in racial profiling and racist remarks, the TO responded that she had "misinterpreted" his comments, asked her if she was too sensitive about race, told her she should reconsider doing police work, and formally told her that a memo about the incident would be "sent up the chain of command and put in her file."[56]

> In 2003 the 7th Circuit Court dismissed a Chicago police officer's case by ruling that "occasional vulgar banter tinged with sexual innuendo [by] coarse or boorish workers [was] not sufficiently egregious to [be] actionable.[55]

Such tactics instill fear in female officers. As a survival skill, they learn to never name a male officer's behavior or language as sexual harassment or discrimination. They learn to overlook, minimize, deny and joke about what is actually offensive and demoralizing. Women have to deal with their embarrassment and humiliation, feelings of powerlessness to do anything about the situation, hopelessness that it will ever improve, rage and depression. Denying their own experience and emotions drains them of physical and emotional energy, and sometimes of their physical health.

When female officers dare to talk about the harassment and/or violence that they experience, they're labeled as radical troublemakers, feminists or lesbians. Some men and women ridicule, threaten or shun those who talk. Such tactics alienate women from other officers—male and female—making them uncertain whom they can trust, so they decide to trust no one. This prevents the women from collectively addressing the harassment or discrimination and ultimately serves to protect male power.

Stripes, stars and bars

Symbols are international nonverbal means of communication which are often used to convey status and power. They may also indicate membership in an exclusive network of individuals. In law enforcement, the uniform, badge and gun are internationally recognized symbols of power and authority—and of membership in the exclusive fraternity of policing. Additional symbols unique to the profession—stars and bars—further indicate an individual's due level of respect and authority—and membership in the more exclusive fraternity of rank. When women and minorities are denied or limited access to such symbols, or limited or denied in their opportunities to qualify and apply for such recognition, or limited or denied permission to form and participate in their own support networks, they are relegated to a second class inferior status.

Historically, women and minorities have been denied or limited in their access to symbols of power in law enforcement. Both women and blacks were required to wear uniforms which distinguished them from "real" officers: blacks wore different color shirts and badges; women wore heels, gloves, skirts and badges which identified them as patrol*women*. Both often received inferior equipment, cars and weapons. Still today, police agencies do not equip female officers with adequate weapons and uniforms tailored to their needs. Police organizations may defend themselves by claiming that manufacturers don't design and produce equipment for women. That is a difficult argument to buy in light of the sophisticated equipment, weapons and clothing that they are able to manufacture *for the men*. Proper-fitting uniforms and equipment are not just issues of appearance, they are life-safety issues.

> *I taught recruits for five years and males seemed to join for the Badge. They are excited by the power and control, status and uniform. They would repeatedly flash their badges at each other after receiving them. I never noticed any female recruits do the same thing.*

> *How embarrassing it is when the vendor comes to measure you for your bulletproof vest. One measurement that they need to take is from nipple to nipple, and the person measuring you is a man. Talk about feeling violated. You have to go through providing cup size, being measured in front of your male peers, often in a briefing room. Of course, the cup size and measurement proves a point of interest for your co-workers. Never once have I had a vest come back to me comfortably fitting. The end result is always a flattening of your breasts despite the efforts by the male-dominated industry to "make a pocket" to cup you comfortably.*

> *I was commissioned as an officer in the early 1980s. When I inquired of our uniform supplier if they carried uniforms specifically for female officers, the man laughed at me. He said, "No, women are just a fad in policing." So, I bought shirts that buttoned on the*

> *opposite side of women's clothes and paid to have them altered. Pants were a nightmare. They had to be altered so much in the waist that my pockets actually met in the back. The alteration costs were also astronomical. I'd like to say that things have changed 25 years later, but I just bought two new pairs of "women's" pants and I had an additional $25 a pair in alterations just to make them fit properly. They are all still cut far too short in the crotch. They just don't fit a woman's body.*
>
> *I was the first female officer to get pregnant. The agency didn't know what to do with me. They made me buy khaki maternity pants and sew a brown stripe on the sides. My maternity uniform shirt consisted of a size 18 male officer's shirt. The tails were cut off and a hem sewn to finish the bottom. I carried my revolver in a purse while I sat the desk sergeant's office and listened to walk-in complaints.*

In order to move up the ranks, an officer requires opportunities for additional training and experience. Such training and assignments however, are not considered a right but a privilege granted by those in power. Coveted assignments such as SWAT, canine and narcotics not only indicate an individual has the appropriate skills, but also the *approval* of the PTBs. They thus become members of an even more exclusive network and have access to even greater power.

While male officers are encouraged to participate in team sports and other male-identified activities, any form of networking for women is discouraged. In many departments it is common for female officers to be assigned to separate shifts and/or locations. A female captain reported how command ensured that the three women in the agency were assigned to separate shifts in separate sites, making certain that they were unable to form any shift time camaraderie. A Sheriff's Deputy was never allowed to work in the same zone as other female Deputies on the same shift. When another female Deputy questioned why this was, she was reprimanded by their sergeant for even suggesting the assignments were discriminatory.[57]

> A committee of female officers from twelve agencies within my state wanted to host a training for female officers on working in a male-dominated profession. We knew that if we mailed a brochure with this title to Chiefs and Sheriffs it would go into "File 13." So, we called it "Female Officer Survival Techniques." Department heads thought it was a tactical training. The course had a huge response and was repeated several times due to the demand through word of mouth.

> I'd like to see more networking so the younger ones have role models to look up to. When [the sergeant] was up, the younger ones said, "Well, if she can make it then why can't we?" It's very important to have networking and role models.

Perhaps surprisingly, networks are the key to individual power. Members of a group—whether formal or informal—are privy to an exclusive information network. They have access to greater knowledge than they could ever achieve on their own. The PTBs know this. Their exclusive networks enable them to remain in power by choosing when and with whom they will share their power. That is why being excluded—even from choir practice—is so damaging to the careers of women and minority officers.

Conversely, it can also be damaging for women and minority officers to take advantage of exclusive department-sponsored mentoring programs. This can create a segregated atmosphere which destroys unit cohesion and reinforces an "us versus them" mentality. Women and minorities are led to believe that their success depends on uniting within their separate classes; white males perceive the programs as practicing reverse discrimination. Those who truly possess the power to change the system are not held accountable for promoting practices that simply perpetuate the status quo. Even memberships in such national organizations as the International Association of Women Police (IAWP), National Black Police Association (NBPA) or the National Center for Women and Policing (NCWP) can result in questions and doubt about an officer's commitment to the "team."

> When I wanted to go to the NCWP conference after being promoted to Commander, my deputy chief told me that they're a radical group that will taint my professional standing if I associate with them. I said the presenters and seminars appeared to be excellent, relevant to an agency working towards increasing the number of females in the department. I also asked him if he had ever attended one of these conferences to validate what he was sharing. He looked at me like I was crazy and said, "You got to be kidding me." He ultimately allowed me to attend. I was awarded a "Breaking the Glass Ceiling Award" at the conference and was very proud of it. When I returned, I tried to express the value of the conference and what I had learned as well as the fact that I had received the award. I was told this was my first and my last NCWP conference that my agency would pay for.

In addition to the recruitment process, each agency perpetuates its own culture and philosophy through its promotion process. Like other institutions, policing perpetuates its culture and philosophy through the promotion of individuals who are likely to maintain and foster the values and culture of the agency. Chiefs and other high-ranking officers are likely to choose, groom and promote candidates based on the similarities to themselves. The chief promotes officers that he can work with—meaning those who think the same way he does, with whom he can communicate, those who see eye-to-eye with him. They thus perpetuate their power and influence. In agencies where the chief or sheriff enjoys the political support of the community, the community also encourages the promotion of individuals who will maintain the status quo.

> *After I was promoted from Lieutenant to Commander, I thought the Chief was paying me a visit to say congratulations. Instead he told me a biblical story of women in history as prostitutes. He pointed out how much I looked like a prostitute he used to know—definitely no congratulations in that conversation.*

Many women have repeatedly been passed over for promotion, but told to be patient and to be "good little soldiers" and their time would come. The promise of future promotion with its conferred authority and recognition gives women and minorities a stake in the system. But the cost is their complicit participation in their individual and collective exploitation. The symbolic rewards of the system are offered in exchange for their compliance with the status quo; those who challenge it are rarely candidates for promotion.

> *When I interviewed for my promotion to lieutenant, the Merit Commission panel was all male. I wore a business suit with a knee-length skirt. As I approached the door, one panelist greeted me. He looked me up and down from head to toe. He said, "That will work fine." I got a perfect score on my interview. To this day, I don't know if it was due to my ability to communicate effectively and answer their questions satisfactorily or because of my attire.*

> *My husband and I put in for the same job—surveillance position within Intelligence Services. He went one day and I went the next. He was asked policing questions, my interview focused on our kids, my responsibilities,*

and whether I could adequately perform the duties required.

Token positions allow institutions to claim that women and minorities have equal opportunity for advancement *if* they are qualified and work hard. Police agencies display their token women and blacks as proof that systemic barriers do not exist—there are simply individuals who can or can't make the grade. Displaying them as examples simultaneously admits and denies the chauvinism that most women and blacks are inferior and cannot make it to the top echelon without special considerations. When they do, white male officers all too often show their resentment by refusing to recognize their rank and overtly or covertly undermine or defy their authority.

You are going to have to accept that the only reason you have gotten as far as you have is because you are a token. They have to have some females in supervisory positions just to keep their funding.

For agencies that are pushing to gain or keep accredited status or are under certain political pressures: you'll see their recruitment pamphlets, commercials, advertisements with the one or two non-white officers constantly being utilized as the token which demonstrates "advertised compliance" to the diversity piece. If you have a black female, you can bet she will be advertised heavily to show that compliance—just don't look any closer at the actual agency make-up.

Many female officers testify that they have to work twice as hard, seek more advanced degrees, receive extra training, and constantly prove themselves, yet superiors still overlook them for promotion because of the brass ceiling. Supervisors sabotage their promotional exams by denying time to train, study or practice. Female officers also are usually dependent on a male for their performance evaluations, which often leads to sexual harassment. Those that make it to higher ranks are often accused of sleeping their way to the top. Some female officers who have career ambitions and are thwarted by the brass ceiling are disappointed in *themselves* rather than in the system. They deny or fail to recognize that systemic barriers exist and believe that they could break through into management if they only work hard enough. "No matter how often a woman proves herself in the job, she's got to do it over and over again," says Diane Skoog, executive director of the National Association of Women Law Enforcement Executives (NAWLEE) and former chief of police for the Carver Police Department in Massachusetts. "Once a guy does it, he's set."[58]

Women and minorities find themselves in aggressive competition with each other because they are vying for a single token opportunity. Rather than being able to bond and support each other, they are alienated from one another. Promotion, once achieved, also sets an individual apart and risks betrayal not only of her core supporters but, ultimately, betrayal of her Self. She may believe that she has a chance to further the interests of her own group through positive example and hopes to proceed without accusations of promoting a race– or sex–based agenda. However, the dominant group (white males) often accuses a woman or a black who uses their position of power to mentor and advance members of their own group of bias and facilitating reverse discrimination.

> "Loyalty to power overshadows other loyalties, including gender and race." In business, after women reach a certain level, they are less likely to want to help other women advance. As association with a certain group conveys more power, newly admitted individuals identify more with the power group. They seek validation and behave more like

them. Holding onto and getting more power becomes more important than loyalty to the other less important groups to which they belong. Not so for the white male: He aligns perfectly with his race and gender group. His loyalties, far from being lessened, are actually reinforced. His personal view is not torn between the power group and "his" people. He is never accused of pushing an agenda by taking care of other white males. Not only is his choice reinforced, but also his entitlement to make that particular choice.[59]

The token woman or minority male who is eligible for or promoted to higher rank will have a challenge just to survive on a day-to-day basis without the support of their troops. The higher up a person goes on the ladder in any organization, the more resentment they get from the majority, and the fewer peers they have for support. Their presence stokes the white male's fear that *his* job, *his* status, *his* wealth, *his* entire lifestyle is in danger. He feels that *they* are taking over and he feels diminished. He doesn't like it, and he wants to do something about it.

It is impossible to separate issues of gender from issues of race, class and sexual orientation. Even a white, middle-class, heterosexual female officer is caught in a multitude of complex double-binds. In seeking acceptance, she may try to mimic male behavior. As one officer explained, they "become more manlike in their attitude and their swearing and aggressiveness/assertiveness, not thinking that they can retain any sort of femininity."[60] Though her behavior is masculine, she is *not* a man, so she is not fully accepted (and probably labeled a dyke.) If her behavior is feminine, male officers reject her as not being tough enough to be a police officer. The men may expect a female officer to be sexually available to them. If she is, they label her a slut; if she is not, they label her a prude, a man-hater or a lesbian. The female officer has to constantly navigate her way through these contradictory expectations and choose what appears to be the lesser of evils, to choose her best survival technique.

> *I have been told repeatedly over the years, "You are just one of the guys." Therefore I was privy to all of the haunting stories of affairs and verbal abuse—not necessarily a perk to be categorized as one of the guys, but it is a piece of the survival if you want to try to stay and be productive, to be a member of the club.*

Covering and coping are survival techniques that enable one to survive while living in a potentially dangerous environment. "The reason racial minorities are pressured to "act white" is because of white supremacy. The reason women are told to downplay their child-care responsibilities in the workplace is because of patriarchy. And the reason gays are asked not to "flaunt" is because of homophobia."[61] The dominant group has power, backed by the threat and/or use of force, to compel others to "cover."

Cynthia Enloe, Research Professor in International Development, Community and Environment (IDCE) and Women's Studies at Clark University, points out we should not confuse women's coping mechanisms with women's empowerment. Coping is a survival technique. Female officers who cope with sexist comments and harassment by ignoring them or laughing them off do so because they understand that they have to "go along to get along." As women, they learned long ago that they can choose to fight some battles against sexism, but they have to choose their battles wisely.[62]

Some women officers adopt a non-threatening feminine role such as that of a surrogate mom, sister, or daughter in an attempt to de-sexualize interactions within the sexually charged environment. When male officers sexualize their interactions with female officers, the women may try to ignore it or take it in stride, resigned that "boys will be boys." They try to believe that if they don't name the behavior as sexual harassment or abuse, it isn't. This, of course, forces them to deny their own perceptions of reality and to tolerate the men treating them as sex objects.

Female police officers who are desperate for acceptance and deny their own vulnerability as women may respond as harshly or judgmentally to other women as male officers do. They may find themselves adopting the men's attitudes, language, actions and behaviors, going so far as to refer to other women as bitches or whores and saying that those who are beaten or raped deserved it. They misdirect their anger to the victim and blame her for the violence perpetrated against her. These female officers fail to hold men accountable for men's violent crimes against women. These officers insist that they are "not like other women." They refuse to acknowledge or admit that they would ever be vulnerable in a situation due to their gender. They pride themselves on being able to handle situations *without* becoming the victim. Meanwhile, while using this survival strategy, they don't realize that they are cooperating with their own oppression.

Others try to survive by aligning themselves with the men, trying to blend in with the dominant group. They internalize the men's devaluation of women, and look at things through the male gender lens. Susan Martin, Wendy Austin and others stress that when female officers try to be one of the boys in order to gain power, they actually lose it. By accepting male standards of policing, they devalue the feminine approach to policing and the feminine perspective. They disempower themselves and other female officers by assimilating into the culture rather than challenging it.

Despite the devaluation, harassment and discrimination they face, many female officers stay in the profession because they love the work. As a former Commander related, "We are good at it, really good. We *do* change the culture, albeit with baby steps." Many believe it is the best job they could have, that it offers better financial compensation and benefits than they could find in the private sector. Many are ambivalent about the culture, but hope that the culture will change; they hope to personally make a difference. Some officers express hope that the incoming young male recruits will not perpetuate their fathers' sexist attitudes, but many female officers are not optimistic. They see no evidence that the young recruits are interested in changing the police culture.

> Agencies recruit males from the general population. A 1997 study found that "over 25% of college males [surveyed] believe that it is appropriate for a man to beat a woman whom he believes to be sexually unfaithful, and that over 10% believe it is appropriate to beat a female partner who repeatedly refuses to have sex."[63]
>
> A 2004 report prepared for the National Institute of Justice found that sexual assault preventive intervention programs may show changes in attitudes and knowledge, but "changes in attitudes and knowledge may or may not result in changes in behavior." Most programs failed to produce significant, lasting changes in attitudes or behaviors.[64]

Although the most blatant barriers to women in police work have fallen, and women are entering policing in increasing numbers, they still encounter an organization that is far from gender neutral. Rather, their options and opportunities for advancement are limited by the gendered work culture; male colleagues who resent and resist their presence as a threat to their occupational solidarity and self-image as men's men; interactional barriers including sexist language, sexual harassment, performance pressures, paternalism, and gender-related stereotypes; and gendered organizational policies and practices that disadvantage women by valuing and rewarding characteristics and qualities associated with masculinity. These barriers and handicaps are built into the gendered work structures and patterns governing male/female interaction and continuously force each woman officer to think like a man, work like a dog, and act like a lady."[65]

Female officers today, like female officers in the past, leave the profession because of the hostile work environment, sexual harassment and discrimination, hazing, exclusion from the informal networks necessary to gain promotions, and the brass ceiling that keeps women in their place and out of the command structure. Some leave because their agency penalizes them for being pregnant and for being mothers. Gender-biased personnel policies, limited assignment opportunities and requirements to work rotating shifts clash with the traditional female responsibilities for child-rearing and/or taking care of elderly family members. Similar to their male colleagues, women also cite occupational stress, dissatisfaction, burnout, performance problems and physical illness as reasons for leaving. But, in addition, surveys reveal that the main reasons women leave policing are gender-specific: devaluation of women, sexual harassment and family care issues.

> Women often leave policing when they become pregnant. Since men think we are taking a job from them anyhow, our male counterparts convince us we can't be a good mother and a cop at the same time. I had an officer tell me I should be home raising my daughter instead of working inner-city patrol. He said I was being neglectful and I wasn't being a good role model for her. As if society in general doesn't make working mothers feel guilty enough.
>
> My daughter was hospitalized in the pediatric intensive care unit when she was under 24 months old. When I telephoned the Chief, he stated, "We can't have you female officers calling in sick every time your child has a cold," and he denied me leave. I informed him I would be absent without leave as I had to be at the hospital with my child. I later filed a complaint with the Human Relations Commission. The allegation of misconduct was dismissed and I received an apology from the Chief.
>
> I know statistics say that the numbers of women who stay in the police are very low. And I can tell you why—'cause it's just too hard. After fighting, fighting, fighting, it's a constant battle.

What is *not* commonly recognized is that many female officers leave law enforcement as a result of abuse by an intimate partner, often another police officer. The attitudes and beliefs of fellow officers and superiors often mirrors that of the abuser. The police culture itself, with its emphasis on obeying orders and respecting (male) authority, serves to condition female officers to tolerate abusive treatment.

Police Domestic Violence on the Radar

Officer-involved domestic violence is particularly problematic because police calls for domestics constitute approximately 50% of violent crime calls. The reality that police officers who batter might be *responding officers* to domestic violence calls in the community is cause for public alarm. Can police agencies or the public rely on an officer who batters to hold a civilian batterer accountable or to protect a female victim from intimate partner violence? Despite laws, policies, protocols and training, might an officer who batters act in accordance with his *own* attitudes and beliefs rather than in accordance with official protocol? Is this another reason why police-perpetrated domestic violence remains hidden—so as to not foster deeper public mistrust?

Because of the relatively few women officers, male officers compete among themselves for the women's attention, especially the newly hired ones. Many women are naïve about the sexual politics and games when they first enter an agency. There may not be any female officers who are willing or able to fill her in or help her adjust to the culture. She may not realize the extent to which she is likely to be the target of speculation, innuendo, gossip and sexual advances.

Many of the male officers put women, including female officers, in categories ranging from "good girl" to slut. Their messages to female officers are mixed, placing a female officer in the classic double-bind: if she wants to be accepted into the group, she's expected to be sexually available to her male colleagues (at least until one of them claims her as "his"), yet if she is sexually available she will be labeled a slut. True to the sexual double standard, a male officer can brag about his sexual exploits and adventures: the more women he's had, the more enhanced his image and status in the eyes of the other male cops. The image and status of a female officer who has had (or is rumored to have had) sex with more than one man, however, is not enhanced in anyone's eyes.

> In the March 1992 *American Spectator,* David Brock described Anita Hill as "a bit nutty, and a bit slutty." The phrase returned for Jones v. Clinton, and the term is now casually used as the "nutty or slutty rape defense."

More than one superior has implied or straight out suggested that I sleep with them. Funny how "No" translates into negative treatment afterwards.

A female Deputy began to reveal that she actually was a lesbian, in order to attempt to stop the romantic pursuits by male Deputies and command staff. While in Court Security, she was forced to continually listen to male Deputies' derogatory statements about lesbian Deputies, particularly those who did not fit a stereotypical "female" image.[66]

Of course, lots of fellow officers expect you are just dying to sleep with them. I have supposedly had affairs with every partner I ever had. But funnier still, I've been rumored to be sleeping with people I have never even met! There's also the hormonal competition to see if they can steal you away from the current male in possession of you. Their stuff is better than the other guy's—just give them a chance and they will show you.

Women cops speculate every time a new cop comes on line. "She's really pretty. Which one of the guys is gonna get to her first?" "New and cute. Who's gonna score?"

Female subordinates who were known to be the unwelcome recipients of a male Correctional Officer's romantic attention (including cards sent to their homes and surveillance of their homes) stated that his behavior was so severe that he had been nicknamed "Walker the Stalker."[67]

If a single female officer consistently rejects sexual advances, male officers may interpret her refusal as evidence that she is a lesbian. Some female officers have even felt pressured into having sex with male officers as the only way to dispel perceptions or rumors that they are lesbians. The accusation that one is a lesbian can be dangerous in a male-dominated profession, leading a woman to be at even greater risk of sexual assault. Many male officers see lesbians as threats to male power because lesbians attempt to live independent of men without the need to obey or submit to them.

> Defaming a woman by sexual reference was once so well-oiled a practice that in 1891, lawmakers in England enacted the Slander of Women Act in an attempt to stem the wrongful ruin of reputations… to offer women wrongfully accused of "unchastity or adultery" a legal remedy.[68]

A woman's refusal to be sexual with men has been sufficient reason for men to question a woman's sanity. Men professionally diagnose such a woman as being "frigid," abnormal, or even insane. Officially, she is not a slut, but she *is* a nut. Once a woman is labeled a nut, she is terribly vulnerable to society's control. She can be isolated, incarcerated, hospitalized, even subjected to physical punishment. Historically, men have had the power and societal permission to "treat" such women surgically, chemically, or electrically under the guise of "curing" them and helping them adjust to their role in society.

Male police officers as a group do their part. A female officer whom they determine to be a slut or a nut serves as an example of what a female cop should not be, and as an example of what happens to a cop whose behavior doesn't fit into the culture.

When a female officer accuses a male officer of sexual assault or battery, the men know that she doesn't have a case if she isn't considered credible—that is, if she can be labeled a slut or a nut. When she files a complaint with Internal Affairs (IA) or a supervisor, they will interview others in the department to get the dirt on her. If the men report that she has "slept around," it is sufficient evidence that she is a slut and therefore not a credible complainant. To prove that she is a nut, they can send her for a psychological evaluation administered by a psychologist of their choosing who may diagnose her as unstable, paranoid, histrionic, "borderline" or, in lay terms, "nuts." The bottom line is destruction of her credibility and thus the destruction of her complaint. When a woman's sexual reputation or her sanity is judged by the male standard, a woman doesn't stand a chance.

The evolution of an abusive relationship

Just because a woman chooses the non-traditional career of policing does not mean that she chooses to give up having a traditional personal life. She may want to be in a monogamous relationship, be married and have children. The nature of the job and the police culture may, however, limit her choice of potential partners. Civilian men may have difficulty understanding the demands of the job. They may be intimidated by her career choice, resent her unpredictable work shifts, and fear the danger she faces daily. She may be attracted to male officers because they share her interest in the job and understand the life commitment it requires. Responding to the pressure in the sexually charged environment of policing, a female officer also may seek a monogamous relationship with a male officer who she believes will protect her from other male officers, help her break through her social isolation, or proclaim her (hetero-)sexual identity. For these and many other reasons, female officers usually end up in intimate relationships with other officers; many marry them.

Many female officers say that they initially had reservations about getting romantically and sexually involved with a male officer because of things they heard about them. Male officers know this, and are well-versed in ways to overcome a woman's resistance. Typically, an officer will assure her that he "isn't like the other guys"—a statement that admits that what she's heard about most male officers *is* true. He tells her that, in contrast to the others, he is sensitive, trustworthy and he doesn't sleep around. He says he isn't threatened by her being a cop; rather he admires her independence and assertiveness.

Despite the image of being strong family men who adhere to the traditional, conservative values of marriage and family, many officers marry and divorce several times throughout their careers. Having been married and divorced two, three, or even four times is viewed as an occupational hazard—at least for male officers—and as such, bears no stigma. Some male officers wear their multiple divorces as a badge of honor that proves that they have not succumbed to the control of any single woman. Multiple marriages and affairs also serve as testimony to sexual prowess and commitment to masculine privilege.

> Police lean to the right politically and morally. They advocate the straight and narrow path to right living… They believe in the inviolability of the marriage vows, the importance of the family, the necessity of capital punishment… But cops do not necessarily abide by the apple-pie-and-motherhood values that they assert… At least half the married male police officers whom Baker [*Cops: Their Lives in Their Own Words*] interviewed told him about their girlfriends and mistresses.[69]

Female officers, however, say that a stigma *does* attach to women who have been married multiple times. And, if a female officer has been in even *one* abusive relationship, her colleagues and supervisors are likely to think that she is a poor judge of character. The police culture, like society in general, blames women who "allow" men to abuse them. The female officer who is victimized even once by an intimate partner may be considered incompetent as a police officer; a series of abusive relationships would likely disqualify her from further consideration.

> *I was B's third wife. I also carried the stigma of being married twice already. I would be even more of a failure*

and further stigmatized if I were to fail at this third marriage.

I was his third wife. He had me convinced that the other two were crazy. He made me dislike them and I did not even know them. As time passed, he would compare me to his other wives by stating I was "no different than the other two." I tried so hard to convince him that I was worthy of his love.

I was selected as the first female in the agency to attend the National FBI Academy. After graduation, I interviewed for a top-level command position. The civilians on the panel were told of my failed marriages and personal background by other command-level personnel who also sat on the panel. The position was awarded to a lower-ranking male with less time on the Agency, less formal education and no advanced supervision training. We cannot compete with our male colleagues even when we have the credentials.

The male officer who is trying to overcome a female officer's resistance will explain to her that his ex-wives were abusive and were to blame for his failed marriages and failed relationships. He claims that the women knew what they were getting into by marrying a cop, but they simply refused to accept the life they chose. Despite all the advantages of being a cop's wife, the women refused to understand him and make the sacrifices necessary to make a police marriage work. Some men claim that they thought the woman was "a good girl," but she turned out to be a slut, sleeping with any available guy. Some claim the ex was a drug addict or alcoholic who neglected the house and kids. Surprisingly many of their ex's turned out to be emotionally or mentally unstable and/or self-destructive. In one way or another, the male officers have always been the victims and their ex's were all, in one way or another, nuts.

He convinces her that she is perfect for him. She has what all the others were missing. She feels sorry about his past experiences with women who have hurt him, and she becomes determined to make it all up to him. He may say that he likes that she's on the job, and she isn't "like other women cops" he knows. Saying this, of course, reveals his negative opinion of women officers, but she probably won't notice. She's happy to hear that she doesn't fit any of the negative stereotypes of women officers, especially if she is new in the department. She may be grateful that he recognizes her for what she is— she *is* exceptional. She is proud of being able to balance her life as both an officer and a woman. He assures her that he sees her as feminine and sexy even though—and maybe because—she wears the uniform and badge. At this point, her higher rank—or her ambitions to further her career—are a turn-on and a challenge, not a threat. Conquering a female cop who is strong, confident, and ambitious requires far more skill than conquering a mere civilian woman, an enticing challenge for a male officer.

A whirlwind romance, quick involvement, excitement, sexual attraction and emotions often prevent the female officer from seeing that the man pursuing her is actually a lot like the other cops he disavows. He wants her to devote all of her free time and energy to him because he is just crazy about her. He calls her, pages and e-mails her several times a day to make sure that she is okay and to let her know he is thinking about her. He wants to know everything about her, where she goes, what she does, who she's with so he can feel close to her. He masks his obsessions and his need to control her by what appears to be simply intense interest, concern and protectiveness.

The competitiveness of the police culture may cause him to see every man, including fellow officers, as potential rivals for his woman's affection. He is not likely to confront his peers if they flirt with or come on to his intimate partner, however, because that would reveal his insecurity. Instead, he may warn her about the vicious cop rumor-mill and urge her to keep the details of their private life between them. He tells her about the way male cops think and talk about women, and he says he doesn't want her to be the object of the other officers' fantasies, gossip, amusement, or the target of their sexual advances. He tells his girlfriend or wife that she'd better "watch herself," and that it would be best if she steers clear of male officers as much as possible.

> *When I came on the job, few women were assigned to patrol the streets. If they were, they had a partner. Every time I was assigned a new male partner, my husband questioned me as if I had already had sex with the new guy. He wouldn't dare approach my partner and ask him, but he had no problem accusing me of something I had not done. I worked hard to get a solo car to avoid these accusations.*

The male officer derives a sense of entitlement from the mere fact that he is a male in a male-dominated society. "Entitlement is the belief that one has special rights and privileges without accompanying reciprocal responsibilities."[70] His position of authority and power as an officer tends to enhance his sense of entitlement to push beyond the limits of the ordinary social roles and norms—after all, *he is the one who enforces them*. The police mystique makes the (male) officer bigger than life; his job is about confrontation and struggles of power between good and evil; it is violent and it is dangerous. A (male) officer who puts his life on the line every day may well believe that he deserves some extraordinary privileges.

One of the privileges to which he feels entitled may be to have the services of more than one woman in his life. He may think he deserves a variety of women to fulfill his variety of needs: a mother, sisters, a wife, daughters, girlfriends, prostitutes and co-workers—all of whom have their proper place in his life. He may depend on the domestic services of his mother until a girlfriend or wife takes over. He may have a wife who is available for sex-on-demand, keeps his house, and raises his kids. He may have one or more girlfriends who provide sex, emotional support and boost his ego, even if he has a wife. He may exploit sex workers on the street in exchange for looking the other way on their illegal activities. Of course, he is careful to keep his women isolated and a safe distance from one another. Many female officers report that the men who freely socialize and joke with them on the job ignore them at social functions when their wives are present. Though he monopolizes his girlfriend's or wife's time, he makes it clear that he needs to spend time with the boys doing guy things like going to choir practice, parties, the occasional strip club and bachelor parties where there are lots of women available. He assures her he isn't into it, he just doesn't want to be out of the group.

> *At work, my male cohorts thought nothing of telling a sexist or sexual joke in front of me because I was supposed to be "one of the guys." They always asked to have coffee and dinner with me and included me in most of the "choir practices." But if there was a function, like the Policeman's Ball where their wives or girlfriends were invited, they didn't acknowledge my presence. I always felt totally shunned and unaccepted at these events, so I no longer attend.*

> I don't want to check my appearance in your eyes... I don't want to be a man. I just want to be what I am... I want to be a real woman.[71]

A female officer may struggle to overcome her life-long conditioning to act and be feminine as she strives to be accepted into the male-identified world of policing. Her deep socialization as a woman may compete with her not-so-deep socialization as an officer. As a result, she may seek to assure herself and her intimate partner that, despite doing a "man's job" she is still a woman. At the same time, she may seek to assure herself that she is as competent as any man to do the job.

Her intimate partner may not respect her as a "real cop" because she isn't a man, and he may not respect her as a "real woman" because she is a cop. Leanor Boulin Johnson addresses these gender-role conflicts: "Gender-work role conflicts arise because traditional female behaviors do not coincide with the tough, assertive behaviors often demanded of a police officer. Often women receive mixed and incompatible messages as to whether they should act like women (feminine, nonaggressive, submissive, courteous, gentle) and demasculinize their roles, or act like typical police officers (tough, aggressive, authoritarian) and defeminize their roles. If they select the latter, their male counterparts may perceive them as "pushy" and "castrating" and their mate and children may perceive them as unloving and callous. Yet, if they choose to act like women, male officers may feel they don't have a partner upon whom they can rely."[72] The conflict between these two extremes can make her feel insecure and inadequate as a woman and as a police officer. Her insecurity leaves her especially vulnerable to manipulation and abuse in an intimate relationship.

The female officer dating another officer understands that the hyper-masculine competitive culture fosters male expectations of the ideal woman, including emphasis on her appearance—her size, weight, shape, clothes, hair and makeup should be flawless. He doesn't want her to look (manly) like a cop. He wants her to look feminine, soft, vulnerable and sexy, and she does her best to look her best at all times. He expects her to be sexually enticing and even buys her alluring clothes and lingerie. Of course, maintaining a serious relationship requires more than simply looking good. He expects his woman to be capable on the home front—to be the perfect housekeeper, cook and mother.

> *I always tried for the androgynous look, but after I was a cop I got interested in wearing feminine clothes and sexy lingerie. I think I tried to overcompensate to prove my femininity to him.*

It may be difficult for a female officer to identify abusive and controlling behaviors in intimate relationships with male officers because the women are expected to, and do, become desensitized to many of the similar (normal) behaviors of the men on the job. This conditioning on the job is likely to result in an increased tolerance of the demeaning, insulting and humiliating behavior of an abusive intimate partner. Though female officers wield the authority of the badge on the street, they are expected to submit to male authority in the department and in the home. Though some say that female and male officers both have the potential to "bring the job home… treating the family like citizens, expecting the last word, doing things by the book, and being overly critical,"[73] the female does not share the male's sense of entitlement to authority within the home or intimate relationship.

> *If I moved anything of his, he'd become unglued. He'd say, "Don't mess with my stuff!" Lots of cops have OCD [obsessive compulsive disorder]. It must come along with the profession. I have to wonder, though, is it OCD, or is it control? I couldn't decorate the house, I couldn't even hang a picture without his approval.*

When she begins to see signs of controlling and intimidating behavior, she maintains faith that underneath his tough macho shield is a tender man and heart that she can reach if she just gives him enough love and affection. She excuses his occasional outbursts of anger. She knows that he is trained to control others through intimidation, aggression and violence, but she is also an officer who has received the same training. She knows she'd never use her training against *him* and she feels certain that he'd never use his training or tactics to hurt or control *her*. She wants to believe they have a loving relationship in which they share a balance of power.

He may tell her that though she may be a cop by profession, and as such is entitled to authority and power when she's on duty, she most certainly is not in a position of authority or power in their relationship. He tells her he knows what is best for him, her and their relationship. If he makes a decision and she questions it, sees things differently, or disagrees with him, he tells her she is stupid, naïve, or crazy. He warns her not to fight him and promises her that if she does, he will win. She gives in rather than fighting him; it's not that important. In this way, he gains power and she loses it.

To compel to an act or choose to bring about by force

Police have the authority to use force, even deadly force, to gain and maintain control over members of society who violate the law or who pose a threat to others. All citizens are subject to the authority of the police. Much of police training focuses on teaching both new recruits and sworn officers the compliance tactics used to gain control over suspects. "On most occasions, however, police change behavior merely by manipulating their subjects' knowledge that officers can always resort to law enforcement if appropriate behavior is not changed immediately. Stated most simply, …good police officers are masters of legal coercion: the art and science of marshaling the authority of their office and their own personal powers to get other people to behave in ways the police define as appropriate."[75]

> Bancroft & Silverman define a batterer as "a person who exercises a pattern of coercive control in a partner relationship, punctuated by one or more acts of intimidating physical violence, sexual assault, or credible threat of physical violence. This pattern of control and intimidation may be predominantly psychological, economic, or sexual in nature or may rely primarily on the use of physical violence."[74]

Male police officers who batter their intimate partners use their professional compliance tactics, which include non-physical tactics, to coerce their victims to comply with their wishes. Just as a good police officer can coerce a suspect into compliance without the use of force, an abusive officer can control his intimate partner without the use of physical violence. Many officers never lay a hand on their victims; they know they don't have to. But, like on the job, everything depends on the circumstances: he might use force once in a while to let his woman know who is in charge. After the violent lesson, a certain gesture, a reference to the last time, a tone of voice, simply a look, may be enough. They also use the same scripted justifications for the use of force in their intimate relationships as they use when defending their use of force on the job. Officers who batter are often skilled in manipulating the entire criminal justice system and using it to their advantage.

Marilyn Frye provides this great example of coercion: Imagine that a robber holds a woman at gunpoint and tells her that she can either give him all of her money, she can scream for help, or she can try to escape. Of course, before he held her at gunpoint, she had no desire to hand over her money to anyone, "but the situation has changed, and now, of all the options before her, handing over her money seems relatively attractive. Under her own steam, moving her own limbs, she removes her money from her pocket and hands it over." Frye points out that the woman's situation did not "just change," but that the man with the gun changed it. What the robber did was to make it so that "of the options available, the one that was the least unattractive or the most attractive was the very act [the robber] wanted the victim to perform. Given those options… taking into account her judgments and priorities, she chooses and acts. The elements of coercion lie not in her person, mind or body, but in the manipulation of the circumstances and manipulation of the options."[76] The benefit of coercive control is that the batterer compels the victim to do something that is against her own interest, while simultaneously making it appear that she is acting of her own free will. Society buys into this when we say that a woman has "made poor choices for herself."

The element of coercion is frequently ignored or dismissed as an element in domestic violence, providing a way to blame the victim for making poor choices or being incompetent to make choices in her best interest. The abuser presents the victim with a range of choices and suggests "for her own good" that she choose the option that he wants her to choose. The consequences of choosing other options are relatively worse. It *appears* that she is making her own choice, but in reality he is forcing her at (literal or figurative) gunpoint to choose his desired option. Later, he (and others) will tell her, "This was your choice."

He tells her that his requirements of her are few and simple. She should be able to manage the house and kids. All she really has to do is simply anticipate his needs and perform—all to his high standards. If she fails to live up to his standards, he lets her know how disappointed he is. He accuses her of having misled him, of having changed since they got married, or of having let herself go after the baby was born. She fears that he is starting to think she is a lot like the other women he thinks so little of, and she uses his criticism as a guide of how to improve herself.

> *After I gave birth to our son, I got dressed up because we were going out. I asked him how I looked. He answered, "Are you comfortable looking like that? You can always tell when a woman's had a baby. Her hips and her butt get big."*
>
> *One time he said, "I never thought I'd sleep with anyone who had a mustache... but on you it's cute."*

> *The closer I got to putting all of the pieces together, the more verbally abusive he became. He continued to become more brazen in front of people too—more put-downs in front of the neighbors, in restaurants, in front of his own friends.*

Like playing "good cop/bad cop" on the job, he uses the psychological tactic of vacillating between Jekyll and Hyde personalities to keep his victim confused and off-balance. He is totally different in public and in private. In public, he acts like everything is fine. When they are alone, however, one minute he is complimenting her and the next he is finding fault with everything she does. He lies to her and then denies having said what he said. He expects her to be attractive and sexy and then accuses her of trying to seduce other men or of having an affair. He calls he a bitch, a cunt, or a whore in an attempt to humiliate, degrade and embarrass her, letting her know that she has no more value to him than any woman on the street or in the department; in fact she is "just like the rest of them." The effect of this is crazy-making indeed causes her to wonder if she is losing her mind.

> *At all the parties I was his trophy, but at home I was just garbage.*

While he feels entitled to know everything about *her* life, emphasizing that intimacy requires there be no secrets between them, he may say that cohabitation or marriage is cramping his style. The daily intimacy of living together threatens his sense of autonomy and freedom, and he requires more "space." If she questions him about what he is doing or whom he goes out with, he reprimands her for being in his "personal business" or he claims to be hurt that she doesn't trust him.

> *I dated my ex for 8 years, never lived with him. When I finally moved in, 6 months after we were married all hell*

> *truly began to break loose. When I asked him where he was going in the evenings or on the weekends because I thought I could spend time with him on the drive, I was told it was none of my business. "Don't you trust me? I just need some space." But he'd apply the interrogation techniques learned for the job at home on me.*

She may be especially sensitive to the accusation that she doesn't trust him, because, in fact, she doesn't. She knows all too well that a lot of male officers have affairs, maintain secret bank accounts, own property that their wives don't know about, rent post office boxes, and have private cell phones. Some gamble, use or deal drugs, participate in buying and selling confiscated goods—all without their wives' knowledge. On the one hand, she doesn't want to be suspicious and controlling; on the other hand, she doesn't want to be gullible or vulnerable. She resists asking questions to avoid an argument, or forces herself to take him at his word. If she does bring up her fear that he will cheat on her, he assures her that he wouldn't be stupid enough to try to deceive her—after all, she knows how cops operate and would be able to read the signs.

> *If you challenge any of their behaviors, you are chastised for not trusting them. The fact that you question their faithfulness must mean you are fooling around, otherwise you wouldn't think to bring it up. But people now tell me, "We saw him out having lunch and dinner with all these other women but we didn't want to stick our noses in his business."*

He might decide to reclaim his turf—his freedom and autonomy on the job. To reach this end he may pressure her to quit. He can use the "for your own good" argument that it is in her best interest to quit; he can give her an ultimatum to choose between him and the job; or he can do everything in his power to ensure that her life is miserable if she remains on the job. He may also want her to be financially dependent on him, decreasing the likelihood that she could afford to leave him.

> *It's either them or me, make your choice.*

If the abuser cannot convince her to quit for her own good, he can sabotage her job performance and ruin any chance she may have for promotion. He can keep her in a state of anxiety, ensuring that she is too emotionally upset and distracted to function effectively. He can chip away at her self-confidence and self-esteem on both the personal and professional levels, wearing her down emotionally and physically by arguing, interrogating and manipulating. He can deprive her of sleep, force her to call in sick or report late for duty. He can damage or hide her uniform or equipment. If he is physically abusing her, he can hit her where the bruises won't show, or he can cause visible injuries that prevent her from going to work.

> *I told him about the [new job position] and he flipped out. He was ranting and raving because I hadn't consulted with him before I made a decision. I told him that I had to make a decision on the spot and I was eager to gain the experience. He was protesting, claiming he was concerned about my safety working in an undercover capacity. It wasn't fair of me to put him through that. He couldn't believe I didn't check with him before deciding.*

> *I'd have to invent stories about how my work equipment got damaged. He shredded my ID card five times. I'd get written up.*

If her supervisor or fellow officers suspect that she is being abused, it might open the door to the department scrutinizing their private life, discovering that he is abusing her and that she has been hiding it. It may raise questions about her fitness-for-duty. On the other hand, if her supervisor is unaware or insensitive to signs of domestic violence, the effects of her abuse may be interpreted as disinterest in the job, unreliability, carelessness, or physical, emotional, or mental incompetence. The abuser is likely to take advantage of this situation by planting seeds of doubt about her mental and emotional stability. He expresses his concern over her erratic behavior to co-workers and supervisors. He calls her or makes her report in to him multiple times a day to demonstrate his concern or to give others the impression that she is hounding him. He may ask fellow officers to keep an eye on her and to report any unusual behavior back to him.

Another way to convince her to leave the job is to manipulate her desire to have a family. He may say that policing is no job for a woman with children and family responsibilities. He knows she wants to have kids, he does too, but not until she is ready to quit working and stay home with them. He says that the job is too dangerous for a woman, especially one who is or wants to be a mother. He exaggerates the risk that their kids' mother could end up being killed on the job. He says that their kids deserve the security and peace of mind of knowing that their mother isn't in harm's way. And, besides the danger, there are the crazy hours that make finding reliable childcare nearly impossible, and her schedule will conflict with the children's needs.

Society, supervisors and fellow officers often share and reinforce the abuser's point of view. The message from everyone is: good women stay at home and take care of their families. Though the modern, enlightened world of policing may deny it, the reality of the police world frequently works against female officers being able to adequately fulfill the dual roles of police officer and mother. Department policies and schedules often serve to sabotage her performance in one or both roles. If she focuses on being a wife and mother first, with the job second, she will be looked down upon as an officer. If she focuses on her career first, she will be looked down upon as a wife and mother. While the male officer receives validation and support for his juggling a career and family, the female officer receives little of either.

The pressure to perform both on the job and at home takes its toll on her. Her abuser tells her that she is disappointing him and she knows she is disappointing her fellow officers, supervisors and herself. She's just never good enough. She thought she was different and could juggle the demands of being a cop, a woman and a mother, but she fears that she can't. But, if she quits her job, she'll lose everything she's worked for. She blames herself and keeps trying harder. She doesn't see that he and the job set her up in a no-win situation. Instead of recognizing that he and the job have ensured that she cannot meet their impossible standards, she feels inadequate that she cannot make the grade in her relationship or in her career.

As he destroys her confidence and self-esteem, and other officers monitor her closely, her performance may decline. She becomes hyperaware of how others behave around her. Fellow officers react differently to her, causing her to act differently, to withdraw, or to be argumentative. She may begin self-medicating her injuries or stress. Her supervisor may call her in for review, put her on probation, or send her for a fitness-for-duty evaluation.

It is common for a victim to be in denial; she doesn't want to believe that her intimate partner chooses to be violent or that his behavior is calculated to hurt her. When he goes into a rage, she wants to believe that he loses control of himself, although she knows from her own training that the use of force is a calculated decision. She searches for other reasons, explanations, justifications and excuses for his behavior; she blames the stress of the job or a particularly gruesome case he is working. She knows she should understand, after all, she's on the job too. She wants to believe that it is temporary, and that it will pass. She wants to be patient and understanding—to be a good wife. Her socialization in the larger society, reinforced by her conditioning in the police culture, may facilitate her acquiescence to the abuser's control and domination. More than anything else, she wants the relationship to work.

> *You've made the investment in the relationship. You are told over and over again, the surprising, aggressive, explosive, abusive behaviors are the direct result of a "bad case" they had to deal with. Over and over and over again.*

As time goes on and the abuse continues, the victim realizes that she is in a significantly different, more dangerous and more vulnerable situation than if she were a civilian. Though she knows that statistically the most dangerous place for a woman is in her own home, she never dreamed that she, as a police officer, would ever be in that vulnerable position. She may have bargained for putting her life on the line as a cop, but she didn't bargain for putting her life on the line when she married one. Contrary to the male officer who enjoys his home as a haven from the job and the streets, her home is not a haven. She feels safer on duty than she does in her own house. She knows that she is expected to fight back on the street, but she is forbidden to defend herself in her home. She realizes that of all domestic violence victims, she may be the most at risk and the least likely to receive police protection. Above all, she doesn't want to be a "victim."

> When a civilian woman married to a cop needs help, she thinks, "...but **he** is the police." When a female officer needs help, she thinks, "...but **I am** the police."

The police culture attaches such a strong stigma to the label of "victim" that being a victim is the antithesis of being an officer. The stereotype of a victim is a vulnerable, powerless, naïve, gullible woman. No woman, especially a police officer, seeks that label. She refuses to identify the violence she experiences as rape, assault, or battering. She may prefer to hold herself responsible for "allowing" it to happen, thus implying that she can control it, she can do something different next time that will prevent an attack. Her denial is a coping mechanism that helps her maintain a sense of control, strength and invulnerability. She simply cannot afford to identify herself or have others identify her as a "battered woman." She fears that others will question how, if she can't even protect herself, she can protect others.

> It is so awful to get the courage up to disclose something so personal and then to be doubted, ridiculed, shunned and shamed by your employer. A fellow officer said to me, "When I first heard, I didn't think that could even be possible because I know you can take care of yourself."

She may want help, but she remains silent because she fears that the consequences of reporting will be worse than the consequences of living with the abuse. She feels alone and doubts that anyone will understand, much less be willing and able to help. The police culture reinforces silence about domestic violence and sexual assault by perpetuating the stigma of victimhood. The culture's ethos of bravery, isolation, secrecy and solidarity (invulnerability and the denial of emotions and reality) forces her to deny her own reality and feelings. The stigma makes it practically impossible for her to reach out for help, thus shielding her assailant.

Female officers have firsthand knowledge about how many officers—male and female—feel about domestic violence, what they say about the victims, how they joke about the calls. She knows that officers frequently sympathize with the abuser, saying things like, "What a bitch! If she were my wife, I'd have hit her, too." She also knows that the "Brotherhood" may protect a female officer "as if she were a sister" when her abuser is a civilian, but not when he is a member of the police family. When he is family, they will probably see things his way, protect him and invoke the code of silence to cover for him. She fears they will see *her* as the traitor, the one who ratted out an officer.

> *After responding to a domestic dispute, the women talk about the victims too. But the men talk about victims like, "He's an asshole, but she's a lunatic too." They refer to them as bitches, sluts, coke whores, dykes, cunts and lunatics. So now I wonder, how would they talk about me if I ever called them?*
>
> *Would I be blamed? Would I be accused of setting up another officer? Would I be viewed as selling another cop down the river? Would I be considered a backstabber? Would I be considered just another cunt that was putting the screws to not only her husband, but a cop?*

Supervisors and co-workers label the officer who makes a complaint as unable to handle her personal problems. The officer taking her complaint may see her as vindictive, interpret her legitimate fear as paranoia, or judge her as over-reacting, too sensitive, or hysterical—all of which have serious career implications. She may feel compelled to risk her personal safety rather than risk her career.

> *The job saved my life because it was the only escape for me.*

If circumstances force her to report, even women officers may resent her and turn against her. They see her as betraying all female officers, and may think reporting domestic violence makes all of them look weak. Some will be sympathetic because they have had similar experiences. Some may be less sympathetic because they have dealt with their own situation in a particular way and believe everyone else should do the same. Others are afraid that showing too much understanding could alert colleagues to the fact that they have been abused, which they may not wish to be known.[77]

> *If women in policing admit to or acknowledge the victimization piece, they are pushed out of the pack—shunned. You want to be able to continue to excel and advance. If you are now a victim, they won't touch you with a ten-foot pole.*

> *The male cops and other female cops treat you like you are contagious. They avoid contact. There won't be any conversation after daily briefing to meet up for coffee, no over-air, "Meet you at ... for a cup." After all, if they associate with you, they may somehow then become a victim or pick up some of the stigma associated with being a victim. It is simply easier to stay away from you.*

> *My personal hell was out on the table for all to speculate about. I knew my peers would label me "A Victim." These words just made me want to scream as loud as I could, "It's okay that this could happen to your sister, your daughter, your friend or anyone else that means*

*something to you? But it's **not** okay because I am a cop? Because I work with you and I deal with these calls the same as you?" I knew there would be speculation, "How could she let this happen? She should know better, she's a cop. What did she do? She must have done something to make him do it. How could she do this to another cop?"*

The cultural stigma attached to the victim label however, does not apply to males who claim to be victims. Though a male officer as victim defies the stereotype even more than does a female officer, many in the system have no trouble believing that a male officer can be a victim. Agency personnel and the courts consistently believe male officers and disbelieve female officers when domestic violence is reported.

He's the "Victim"

Batterers react differently in the aftermath of a violent confrontation with their partner/victim. Batterers' reactions may also change over time as the abuse escalates. Some batterers are remorseful and others never apologize. Some promise never to lay a hand on her again, others threaten murder the next time. Interestingly, the officer who batters a civilian woman begs her not to call the police because that will jeopardize his career; the abuser of a female officer warns her she will lose *her* job if she reports. Some deny the abuse and say it is "all in her head." Others dare the victim to call the police, saying he will simply tell them that she provoked him or that she initiated the violence. He tells her that none of the cops like her, or they all know she's crazy; no one will

> Intimate partner violence is primarily a crime against women. In 2001, women accounted for 85% of the victims of intimate partner violence and men accounted for approximately 15%. Intimate partner violence made up 20% of violent crime against women and only 3% of all violent crime against men.[78]

believe her. He reminds her that his buddies on the force will support him and will sympathize with him—they all feel vulnerable to women who can make accusations of abuse and ruin their careers.

"The higher a batterer's level of entitlement, the greater his apparent perceptual tendency to reverse abuse and self-defense. The typical batterer defines his abusive behaviors as efforts to protect his own rights and defines his partner's attempts to protect herself as abuse of him."[79] When the abuser senses that his victim is going to tell someone about the abuse or report him to the department, he uses this threat to justify taking preemptive action. Just as an on-duty officer who perceives a threat doesn't wait until he is under attack to protect himself, an officer who batters doesn't wait until his victim reports him to take action.

> *The attorney informed me that my husband had called him earlier that day and said that I had assaulted him. That "I was out of control, I snapped, he'd never seen anything like it before," that "I was not myself and something was terribly wrong." Based on that information, it appeared clear to me that my husband realized that I was serious about not covering for him anymore. It seemed to me that he was trying to cover his ass before I filed a police report.*

One preemptive strategy is to file a police report in which *he* claims to be the victim. He may file a report explaining that because he anticipates that his partner is going to make false allegations against him, he wants to get his side of the story documented. He may say that he's concerned about the kids, but doesn't want to make any formal charges against her. He appeals to the reporting officer to keep it all quiet because he doesn't want it getting around the department. "He still loves her, but..." This gives him the opportunity to present himself as the concerned father and aggrieved spouse while painting the victim as being emotionally unstable, jealous, vindictive, or aggressive. He can claim that she *may* be abusing the kids, or filling their minds with lies about him. He can claim that she's been drinking excessively, acting erratically, and that there's even been times when he's had to restrain her from hurting herself. He says he's doing all he can to control the situation, but it may be getting out of hand and he just wants someone to know. Her credibility is undermined before she has a chance.

> *He said, "She could go from moments of calm to rage in a matter of seconds." No truth whatsoever but this was the picture he was painting of me for others.*

The abuser may also be able to manipulate the responding officers into believing that he was assaulted or provoked into striking the victim. He may meet the officers outside the home appearing calm but embarrassed while she remains in the house uncontrollably crying or shouting profanities. He may sign a criminal complaint that results in her arrest, giving him grounds on which to obtain an order of protection. Getting an order may give him the additional advantage of having temporary custody of the children and temporary sole possession of their home. The arrest humiliates and embarrasses her and proves that he is able to mobilize his network of power against her despite the fact that she is also an officer. It is a chilling shock for her to realize that she has gone from being a law enforcement officer to being an "offender."

The arrest of the victim serves to validate what the abuser has been telling their family, friends, neighbors and colleagues about his partner. He can use the arrest to bolster his accusations against her, pointing out that the arresting officers and a supervisor all determined that there was probable cause to make an arrest. Her arrest can tip the scales in his favor with other parties as well: the divorce attorneys, other officers and supervisors, the prosecutor, judge, therapists, child services, school, day-care, the guardian-ad-litem, all of whom may have considered them both equally credible and stable police officers—before her arrest.

> *You've heard of "Driving While Black?" Well, how about "Driving While Victim?" Anytime I currently see a Sheriff's car, I get a skin tingle and crawl, turn a little pale and I wasn't even arrested, I was the victim. I just know they were "his" force.*

Her arrest also seriously compromises the victim's future safety. The abuser now has additional power over her. He has proven that he can have her arrested. Out of fear of being arrested again, she won't dare tell anyone about his continuing abuse. She now understands what it means that it is her word against his, even though she is an officer too. Since she was the one arrested, it will be difficult to convince anyone in the criminal justice system that she is actually the victim.

Most fellow officers, supervisors and judges fail to identify the male officer's preemptive actions as tactics of abuse. They are sympathetic to his situation because his livelihood could be at stake. Few question why he would anticipate that his partner is going to make false allegations or file a false police report against him. The assumption that women commonly lie about abuse is outrageous. The prevailing perception is that all it takes is a woman to report abusive conduct and the alleged perpetrator will be out of a job. In reality, female officers have little credibility when they accuse male officers of sexual assault or battery. If female officers *did* have credibility and a network of powerful relationships, and if there was *not* a double standard, they *would* have the power to do what males have always been able to do—ruin women with rumor, gossip, innuendo and allegations. Female officers wouldn't need proof, just as male officers don't need proof. A woman's word would be enough, just as a man's word is enough.

> *Male officer-abusers have "instantaneous credibility" which is not so for female officer-victims. Our recollection of events is repeatedly questioned. If it was really that bad, an officer especially would have known what remedy to take early on.*

The word of a female officer may be accepted in police reports and court testimony when she is acting in her official capacity. When she is acting for herself, however, it is her word against that of a male officer and she enjoys no such credibility. Her perceptions, memory and interpretation of facts and events are all questionable. Her evidence of abuse, her personal documentation are suspect. When she relates his erratic behavior and lies, she is asked for proof. Gender takes precedence over her professional status when she makes a report or testifies against a male officer.

> *If you are such a good actress at work, if you're able to project happiness and stability, then when you disclose the abuse, they suspect you are lying about it.*

> *My fellow officer asked, "Why wouldn't you have said something sooner if this was really what was going on?"*

The male officer retains his credibility whether he is acting in his professional or personal capacity. When he tells his side of the story, no one questions his memory or his interpretation of the event. His detailing of his partner's character flaws and emotional instability (such as crying or yelling) are accepted as fact. Reflective of the larger society, male status and power in the world of policing ensures that the word of a male officer has much more weight and credibility than the word of a female officer. The male officer who batters is confident that the department will not question his sanity, will not doubt his credibility, will not scrutinize his behavior, and will not judge him as being weak, whining or incompetent when he reports that he is a victim of abuse. Because the police department is his domain, supervisors are unlikely to accuse him of embarrassing the department by bringing his personal problems to the workplace, nor will fellow officers ostracize or harass him for filing a domestic violence report against a female officer. They will understand.

> *Once the agency is aware, the ability of the victim to make credible safe decisions while on the job is under scrutiny. Her decisions are questioned because, "women are so emotional, she likely can't handle the balance of DV disruption and work."*

Though many male officers ridicule female officers for using words when they should use force, they readily believe that a female officer will quickly resort to the use of violence against her intimate partner. They also believe she is able to instill fear in him, despite his relative size, strength, skills and training. They believe she will even provoke a physical fight with him. Believing that a female officer is the aggressor in her intimate relationship contradicts their objections to women in policing: women avoid confrontation, they are not aggressive, and they back down from physical fights. Another common criticism is that women are too compassionate, too sympathetic and too emotional. Yet, this does not apply when it comes to her spouse or lover. Here she is accused of being unemotional, tough, aggressive and willing to inflict pain on the person she loves. Men, on the other hand, are in control of their emotions—except when it comes to passion, love, or jealousy. These emotions in a man are often cited as justifiable causes of beating or even killing a woman who does him wrong.

The department may not believe a female officer can be a victim because she is able—or should be able—to defend herself. The abuser taunts her with, "You're tough, you do a man's job, protect yourself." Yet, if she does defend herself, she becomes vulnerable to the abuser's allegations that she initiated the violence. The abuser may goad her into fighting back or into drawing her weapon so that he can claim self-defense. She knows better than to compete with him on strength or skill. She knows that if she fights back, he will interpret it as a green light to escalate his level of force. His ego and his sense of masculine superiority require him to prove to her that he is stronger, smarter and tougher than she is, so he will do whatever he has to do to win.

> *I could choose to physically engage him or retreat. It didn't take long for me to learn that if I fought back, my injuries would be so severe I wouldn't be able to report for duty. Either the injuries were visible on my face, neck and/or hands or I would be walking with a limp or suffering pain from him kicking me in the abdomen, back, or legs. He would never let me believe that I could be a match for him in a fight. He would always one-up me. However, if I refused to fight I was still emotionally battered by his ugly words. He spewed loudly that I was "worthless" and "pathetic," "couldn't even take care of myself at home" and that I was "wasting a man's job."*

> *When the rumors spread about the domestic violence within my home, a lot of people suggested that I was just as likely to engage in the physical assaults because of my willingness to engage in a physical confrontation on the street if the situation warranted it. So, my assertiveness on the job in dealing with offenders was*

> *compared to my actions in my intimate relationship in my home with my abuser.*

If she does fight back, a female officer can anticipate that the department may determine that she was not justified in using force against her abuser. Or, she may be afraid that the department will categorize the incident as "mutual combat" and hold them both equally responsible and accountable for the incident. They will use the fact that she was able to fight back to prove that she is not a victim. They can justify holding her responsible by claiming that they are avoiding gender bias by treating both parties equally.

> *Overall, I think officers expect that since you are a cop and receive all the self-defense training you would never be a victim. But you know that if you defend yourself, you are going to end up going to jail, not the sweet-talking, poor man who has to put up with the raggy, emotional woman.*

Prosecutors, chiefs, investigators, supervisors, responding officers and fellow officers all believe that these deceitful and manipulative women can easily dupe male officers who consider themselves to be excellent judges of character. These male officers pride themselves on knowing human nature and being able to easily read people. Yet they excuse their pattern of getting involved with one crazy woman after another simply with: *all women* are basically nuts or sluts. In their misogynistic view, it is not men's judgment that is faulty, but women themselves. The explanation for a female officer's involvement with one abusive male after another is not that *all men* are trouble, but that she does something to attract the aberrant violent man. They conclude that "some women just never learn their lesson" or they write them off saying, "some women just like that sort of thing." In private they agree that the female cop is such a bitch that they can understand why her partner hits her.

If she's so crazy, how did she pass her psych eval?

Network of Power

Though domestic violence in the general population has been on the radar for some 30 years, domestic violence in the police population remained off the radar until a blip occurred in 1996. In that year, a bill was attached to the Omnibus Consolidated Appropriations Act of 1997 which removed the exemption from the Federal Gun Control Act of 1968 for military and police who have been convicted of an act of domestic violence. Similar to the Title VII "joke," pro-gun legislators had "removed the military and police exemption in an attempt to defeat the bill as originally proposed. The approach failed and the bill passed as part of an all-night legislative hearing conducted by a Congress desperate to pass an appropriations bill to avert a government shutdown."[80] If a military or police officer had a qualifying misdemeanor conviction on his record, he would no longer be allowed to own a weapon or ammunition unless he had secured a pardon or had his record expunged.

These changes caused havoc in the law enforcement community. Because the bill was retroactive, agencies had to comb through personnel records to ensure that officers who had prior convictions were not in possession of agency-issued weapons. Some argued that the retroactivity of the law unfairly penalized officers who had pleaded guilty to misdemeanor charges years ago when domestic violence was no big deal. They said that in the past, officers routinely pleaded guilty to avoid prolonged litigation.

In response, Penny Harrington (director of NCWP and former Portland OR police chief) said, "police have gotten around the law by routinely getting domestic violence convictions expunged from their record or by pleading to lesser crimes than domestic violence. 'Right after the law came out,' Harrington said, 'there was this huge rush, nationwide, of officers running in to get their records expunged. And most of the judges went along with it.' Harrington blames the entire justice system for the ease with which cops get their records expunged. 'The judges are in league with the officers,' Harrington said. 'Judges also are guilty of family violence, and it always gets covered up. Any high-profile person—a judge, a politically appointed or elected official, or a district attorney—the whole system covers up for each other on this issue more than anything... The prosecutor's office has the right to object to the process, but the final say on expungement is the judge's alone. Once the record is expunged, court documents and police incident reports are sealed and removed from public view.'"[81]

Police Officer-Perpetrated Domestic Violence Research Results 1991–2005
- Johnson 1991: 40% reported they had lost control or behaved violently toward their spouses[82]
- Neidig et al. 1992: approximately 25% reported they personally engaged in violent behavior[83]
- LAPD 1997: 40% of reported DV cases sustained[84]
- Bergen et al. 2000: 6% of Vermont police chiefs report domestic violence incidents by officers[85]

- Campion 2000: New York City – 9% arrest rate and 4% suspension rate for domestic violence; Detroit – 1% complaint rate[86]
- Klein & Klein 2000: 5% self-report as perpetrators, 7% self-report as victims[87]
- Johnson 2005: 40% reported they had gotten out of control and behaved violently towards their spouse in the prior 6 months[88]

"This research demonstrates domestic violence in policing does not exist as an anomaly, but as a cause for serious concern."[89]

There have been appeals to overturn at least parts of the law, but so far none have succeeded. Politically, of course, it was awkward to argue that an officer who beat his wife or girlfriend should be exempt from the gun law. A representative of the Chicago Fraternal Order of Police insisted that the law was unfair because it singled out police officers to lose the "tools of their trade" if they were convicted.[90] Many feared the loss of a substantial number of police officers as a result since studies conducted in 1991 and 1992 showed that between 27% and 40% of officers *self-reported* that they had perpetrated domestic violence. Even using the more conservative domestic violence statistics in the general population (a 30% rate), police officials feared that up to 70,000 officers were at risk of losing their jobs.[91]

However, an *Akron Beacon Journal* survey of the country's 100 largest police departments "revealed few police officers have been forced to give up their guns. The survey, asking each city's police chief how many officers were fired or reassigned to administrative duties as a result of the so-called Lautenberg Amendment, showed that disciplinary actions were taken by six cities and that a total of 11 officers were affected."[92]

More recently, Lonsway *et al.* reported, "the Bureau of Alcohol, Tobacco, and Firearms (ATF)—the federal agency with sole authority to enforce the Lautenberg Amendment—recommends only a small number of cases for prosecution each year and an even smaller number ultimately result in conviction. According to the Public Affairs Office of the ATF, the number of cases forwarded for prosecution under the Lautenberg Amendment during the last few years was 168 in 2000, 169 in 2001, and 201 in 2002. Yet the number of cases that resulted in conviction either in state or federal court was 41 in 2000, 44 in 2001, and 71 in 2002."[93]

In April 1997, seven months after the passage of the Lautenberg Amendment, the International Association of Chiefs of Police (IACP) held the first of several summits to work on crafting a Model Policy on Officer-Involved Domestic Violence. The policy was released in April 1999 and revised in 2003. As with their model policies on other police issues, the IACP encouraged departments to adopt their policy and tailor it to meet the needs of their individual agencies. Having a policy provides guidelines to ensure a consistent police response to the public, relieves responding officers from the peer pressure to collude with the alleged offending officer, promotes victim and officer safety, and protects agencies from lawsuits. A policy on police-perpetrated domestic violence would also demonstrate to the public that the agency was acknowledging the problem and attempting to police their own. However, as of 2003, a national survey of 100 large police agencies found that only 29% had adopted officer-involved domestic violence policies.[94] Many have strong convictions that the department has no business interfering in officers' personal lives. The department may already control many aspects of an officer's off-duty conduct, but meddling in a male officer's intimate relationship is, in their opinion, where they have to draw the line.

When a woman reports that a male police officer assaulted or battered her, the network of power functions very efficiently. Making a complaint against a police officer is a dangerous act, especially when the complainant is herself an officer. The victim puts herself at risk of retaliation from her abuser, from other officers and from the department. The female officer knows that being a member of the police family might protect her if her abuser was a civilian, but the family won't protect her against a male "family" member. The abuser calls upon his network of relationships for support and defense against the allegations. Police-perpetrated domestic violence, like other types of police brutality, could not occur without implicit or explicit approval of other officers, supervisors and ultimately the chief.

> *Time after time people would say, "I'll talk to him and make him stop." His bosses, my boss, the Justice of the Peace, the Crown Attorney. I kept saying this just feeds his feeling of power and his sense that rules do not apply to him. Too much professional courtesy provided to him but never to me.*

Though it may be true that the majority of officers do not commit violence against women, there are those who do. Rather than confronting the abuser, other officers wittingly or unwittingly collude with him in countless ways. They might ignore the abuser's behavior or pretend not to notice. They might acknowledge it but do nothing to stop it. They might bolster his intimidation of the victim by helping him keep her under surveillance, reporting her whereabouts, relaying the abuser's messages to her, and/or harassing her when she is on- or off-duty.

Officers loathe having to respond to a call at the home of an officer. Responding officers are in a doubly awkward position when both the perpetrator and victim are officers. If the department has no particular policy or protocol on officer-involved domestic violence, the strong pressure to abide by the code of silence may cause the responding officers to cover up the incident by not documenting the call. If the department does have a protocol, it probably requires the responding officers to call a supervisor to the scene to relieve the responding officers of peer pressure to abide by the code. However, some supervisors also abide by the code and simply reiterate what the responding officers have already said. The supervisor may attempt to dissuade the victim from making a complaint, suggesting that she think about the implications for *her* career.

> I couldn't understand why no pictures had been taken of me. If the officers had done their job by documenting photos of me, at least there would have been physical evidence. Unfortunately, not only did the officers not properly document the evidence that evening, but they did not even gather the facts or weigh the physical evidence to draw their conclusions. They took the primary aggressor's word for gospel.

Responding officers might refuse to arrest the abuser when there is probable cause to arrest, or arrest him while simultaneously apologizing for doing so. As one commander related, the arresting officer says something like, "I don't agree with having to hook you up because I'd feel the same way you do, but the law these days doesn't give me a choice. I have to arrest you." Intentionally or not, the responding officer thus colludes with the abuser. In a different scenario, the abuser might be able to manipulate the officers into arresting the victim based solely on his allegations.

If an incident results in a departmental investigation, fellow officers may protect the accused by applying the skills and tactics they use in court proceedings. They answer only the question that was asked and do not volunteer supplemental information. If the investigator fails to ask the right questions, he or she won't get the information. Officers employ the strategy of avoidance by saying, "I don't recall;" "I wasn't there." Walker talks about how "the code of silence, through which officers refuse to testify against other officers, has been a major obstacle to eliminating police misconduct. The Christopher Commission report on Los Angeles police officers states, "It is basically a nonwritten rule that you do not roll over, tell on your partner, your companion. In this respect, the police subculture is an obstacle to the development of police accountability."[95]

Some chiefs use the concept of the police family to foster a paternalistic attitude toward female officers. A male chief might say, "My female officers are just like daughters to me." He may suggest that male officers think of the female officers "as if they were their sisters." The use of such labels suggests an intimacy that is inappropriate in a professional environment. It sabotages the female officers' due respect as women and as *officers* and serves to perpetuate sexist attitudes in the police culture. This is not to say that chiefs should ignore the existing sexism and imbalance of power between male and female officers. It is to say that the chiefs have the power and authority to effect change in the attitudes of their subordinates.

Because the chief sets the tone for the department, it is alarming to hear chiefs say things that reinforce the idea that male and female officers have equal power in their intimate relationships or that the female officer is to blame for the male officer's use of violence. Clichés like "It takes two to tango," or "She's no angel" and asserting that the female officer should be able to defend herself perpetuate the myths about domestic violence.

> *The chief admitted to me that he knew. He saw my black eyes. But he also said I was so "inventive." He did suspect, "but then again… You're an adult, if you're being battered, it's up to you to tell us."*
>
> *The vast majority of officer-involved cases begin and end with, "There are two sides to every story. All we have is a he said/she said and there's not enough evidence to sustain the complaint."*

Many chiefs and supervisors are aware of the existence of domestic violence among their own, even though many adamantly deny it. They deny that the code of silence exists, too, and insist that if they had an officer who was an abusive cop, they'd know about it. But, when a situation comes to public attention, the chief is willing to acknowledge that there really *is* a code of silence among the officers, and that is the reason the supervisors were ignorant of the situation. Since the department's liability depends on what they knew, when they knew and what they did about it, ignorance is protection. "Ignorance of subordinates'

> The Code of Silence demands full and total participation. It is the price of admission and by accepting it, as all do—even those destined to rise in the ranks or who are already there—they become tainted… Policing becomes a sort of permanent, floating conspiracy of insiders against the larger public without.[96]

activities… benefits police supervisors… It is common to hear supervisors tell their subordinates that they "really don't want to know about it," to "just keep me out of it," or "just so I don't hear about it."⁹⁷

> *The chief didn't want to know because he wouldn't know what to do. Send me to a local domestic violence agency? Great. I work with them, so what then?*

A direct supervisor who doesn't want to know the details of a specific incident from the reporting female officer can blatantly or subtly communicate that she'd better stop bringing her personal problems to work, and warn her not to become an embarrassment to the department. The supervisor can communicate to the male officer that he'd better "take care of things at home." The woman gets the message that she should keep her private life private. The male gets the message that he needs to get back in control at home. The message to both is that they had better handle it themselves or the department will intervene.

Each tier of the chain of command serves as a layer of insulation for those higher up. Supervisors at each level are responsible for deciding what information needs to be forwarded up to the next level of command. Supervisors are expected to have the ability or talent to handle things at their own level and to demonstrate sound judgment regarding what superiors need to know.

An investigation into an officer's misconduct risks the discovery that department officials have ignored or colluded with the abusive officer and/or his direct supervisors. They, too, have an investment in "making it all go away." In some cases, it becomes essential for higher-ups to protect the abuser and his direct supervisors in order to ultimately protect themselves. The more *their* reputations or jobs are at stake, the more important it is to defend the officer and discredit the complainant. If they do not succeed in discrediting the complainant, they could have to answer to the PTBs and the public for not having taken the appropriate action sooner.

> *During our violent relationship, he never seemed concerned about losing his job. Instead, he constantly threatened me with the loss of my career. He told me that if anyone ever found out about our "hitting each other" that I would lose my job. I was not hitting him... I was always defending myself from an attack. So, when I was forced to call the police because of the level of violence and fear for my life, his threats seemed to come to fruition. I was ordered into counseling because I was "unfit for duty."*
>
> *My chief disciplined me for "failure to keep my private life unsullied" when I reported the violence.*

The prevailing attitude of department personnel may coincide with what the abuser has told his victim—that she should be able to handle her own problems—and the abuse is *her problem*. Many supervisors and chiefs who don't want to know about it may perceive the act of reporting abuse as more of an affront to the badge than the abuse itself. When a female officer dares to report what a male officer is doing to her, she may learn that the department is more interested in preserving and protecting individual and collective male privilege and power than in protecting their female officers.

> *Female officers are punished for speaking out about these issues. Policing, no matter what they profess, still has a strong "old boys club" and a strong aversion to airing any dirty laundry. The only time the public hears about it is if some other organization hears about it and exposes it.*

Plausible Deniability

Department policy may mandate officers to report knowledge of officer misconduct. If the policy does not exempt victims of domestic violence from the mandate, the victim has to choose between jeopardizing her safety and her intimate relationship by reporting, breaking the code of silence by ratting on a cop, or violating department policy by not reporting. If she violates policy by not reporting, she is vulnerable to discipline later if the abuse comes to the attention of the department. She could be punished even though she may not have identified the behavior as "abuse" or had not yet broken through her own denial. The victim also has to try to predict when the investigator will consider the appropriate time to make a report. Does she report "early warning signs" or does she wait until a physical incident? She is taking a risk if she reports the abuse too early or if she waits too long.

> *My own chief went to the Commander and said, "You know people are going to have issues with her credibility because she didn't call the police until the next day."*
>
> *They asked me, "If it was so bad, why didn't you just leave sooner?"*

Though the department policy may advise intimate partners to report warning signs of abuse to allow early intervention and prevention of physical abuse, the investigator may fail to recognize warning signs by interpreting the behavior as normal. Some departments refuse to take reports of non-physical abuse, even though "there are other abuses that, while they don't physically injure anyone, might be termed degrading, dehumanizing, or humiliating. Police departments around the country record these types of complaints under a variety of terms such as verbal abuse, discourtesy, harassment, improper attitude, and ethnic slur."[98]

Despite a department's policy to accept *citizens'* complaints about nonphysical abuse by an officer, the same agency may refuse to accept complaints about identical behaviors when the complainant is the officer's intimate partner. She can report that he flies into a rage, screams and swears, interrogates her, searches through her private space, records her calls and threatens to blow her brains out, but the department doesn't consider these actions "abuse."

> The follow-up question is always, "But, did he hit you?"

If it has gotten to the point of physical abuse, she has to decide what she wants to divulge in her statement. She knows that certain types of severe abuse may possibly result in the department confiscating the abuser's weapon during the investigation, and she fears he will retaliate against her for the department's action. Because of this fear, she may not include the more serious incidents in her statement. She may be in trouble if this information comes out later.

> The department taught me how to lie. I had two polygraphs asking me if I was a victim of domestic violence. I said no. I passed both of them. I said my bruises were because I was athletic, not because he hit me.

> As time went on and it was obvious that his abuse was escalating, I was forced to contact the police department. Each time I had to make contact with the police regarding my husband's conduct, I had to very carefully weigh how I reported his actions and take into consideration keeping myself safe, all other members of the Police Department involved, and particularly my husband's career. The last consideration was the most

> *difficult task to handle because his career could have been jeopardized unintentionally.*
>
> *I didn't believe he would actually ever hit me again. There was too much for him at stake, his career, potential jail time, his children, his family, his reputation.*

In a small department, the abused officer will have to report to her supervisor or the chief. In a large department, she will report to Internal Affairs (IA). She knows that it will make a difference which officer takes her complaint, who investigates her allegations, when she makes the report and what she includes in her report. She may dread opening her personal life to the department's scrutiny because the investigation may reveal details about her life that she would prefer to keep private.

She may have heard through the grapevine that her department handles complaints in such a way as to effectively avoid subsequent complaints. A department's zero tolerance policy may translate to zero tolerance for reporting abuse

> No outside review… has found the operations of internal affairs divisions in any of the major U.S. cities satisfactory… Sloppy procedures and apparent bias in favor of fellow officers combine to guarantee that even the most brutal police avoid punishment for serious violations until committing an abuse that is so flagrant, so unavoidably embarrassing, that it cannot be ignored.[99]

and/or zero tolerance for sustaining a complaint. Supervisors convey the message, "If this is going on, don't let us know about it, because if we do, there will be hell to pay." When the victim is a police officer, more often than not it is she who will pay.

Amongst this oral history is also the awareness of the outcome of previous investigations. The victim has become marginalized or vilified, and is not supported. The perpetrator's career ultimately prospers. It is in this environment that a victim is ordered to report... A victim... [will] be loathe to further endanger their career or personal security by reporting. The specter of punitive action for failing to report only further isolates the victim. They will not seek out the support of a peer, fearing to put them both at risk for punitive measures. The victim becomes effectively cut off.[100]

A female Correctional Officer sent the Sheriff an e-mail describing the continuing hostile environment and retaliation she was experiencing at work. In violation of Department policy, the Sheriff did not document, investigate, or take corrective action on this report. Instead, he wrote an e-mail that stated that it was his position that she had been treated fairly and appropriately and for her own good she should leave this issue and move forward.[101]

Her Lieutenant placed a female Correctional Officer on Administrative Leave for a series of decisions that he deemed "lacked common sense and good judgment." This was the only time in her professional career that she had been placed on Administrative Leave for disciplinary reasons. The same Lieutenant then placed her on a Performance Improvement Plan. Prior to this, she had always been rated Outstanding and Above-average by her superiors and had never received any formal disciplinary action whatsoever. Her Performance Evaluations contained the lowest ratings she had ever received in over 13 years of employment, and she believes they are the direct result of her prior sex discrimination, harassment and retaliation reports and not her actual work performance. The end result: after being placed on Administrative Leave, placed on a Performance Improvement Plan, and subjected to an

Internal Affairs investigation, the Department actively terminated her employment.[102]

In a small department, there is a high probability the investigating officer is a friend or even a relative of the accused. Agencies that have internal affairs units generally rotate officers from other assignments in and out of IA. Investigators are fellow officers raised in the police family, indoctrinated into the same culture, and with the same training and conditioning as the abuser and the victim. The victim may know that the investigator shares the same perspective and attitude as her abuser and is predisposed to see things his way.

The investigator may or may not be familiar with the dynamics of domestic violence or the nuances of *police-perpetrated* domestic violence. Some investigators, whether or not they have had training on the dynamics of domestic violence, remain unsympathetic to victims and loyal to their brothers. Even a female investigator who is sympathetic to the victim may be torn between "thinking like a woman" and "thinking like a cop." Due to lack of education or sexism, many are manipulated by the abuser into buying the familiar litany of excuses and justifications—it's the stress of the job, the boss has been giving him a hard time, he was drunk, he's been working long hours, she nags and provokes him. The investigator may not identify the officer as a batterer, even when it is blatantly obvious.

> Domestic violence perpetration involves a definable and identifiable pattern of attitudes and behaviors. Batterers share key characteristics... The battering problem has unique etiology and dynamics and cannot be reduced to any other cause such as substance abuse, mental illness, or violent personality type. Effective assessment and intervention with families affected by domestic violence

requires a grasp of the central elements of the battering pattern.[103]

Investigators control investigations. Though they are supposed to be strictly objective fact-finders, there is inherent subjectivity; the investigator has to select, piece together and interpret the facts he or she finds. The investigator decides what is significant to the investigation, chooses whom to interview and whom not to interview, what questions to ask and what questions to avoid, and selects what will be included in or omitted from the report. As the investigators weigh the facts, many factors may influence their judgment—not the least of which is the best interest of the department and particular department supervisors. Politics are often involved.

The investigator's job is to hear both sides of the story, and it is crucially important *how* the investigator hears and interprets them. The batterer and the victim typically experience and explain the same situation in very different terms. What the male may dismissively call "just a push or shove," the female may experience as a prelude to escalating violence. What he might have experienced and refer to as "making love," she may have experienced and refer to as sexual assault or rape. When the batterer learns what she said in her statement, he may vehemently deny that the incident ever even occurred.

If the investigator is inclined to believe that the incident did occur, he or she may ask the victim about the circumstances in which the incident took place, and may focus on finding out *why the officer did what he did*. The investigator's questions may reveal victim-blaming attitudes with questions like, "What were you doing to him at the time of or before the incident? What did you do to provoke him? Had you been drinking; were you intoxicated? Were you out of control? Were you being belligerent? Are you going through a divorce? Are you trying to take his kids away from him? Are you trying to ruin his career? Are you seeing someone else? Are you playing games?" Depending on the investigator's interpretation of her answers, he or she may judge the batterer's behavior according to the "reasonable man" or "reasonable cop" (male) standard: *Did the officer react the way any reasonable man would react under the same circumstances?* Underlying all these questions is the assumption that under certain circumstances, battering is justifiable.

If the abuser admits his behavior, he is likely to use the same scripted defenses and justifications that he would use to defend his use of force on the job. He talks about his state of mind during the incident, claims that he felt threatened, that he believed he was in danger, that she provoked, threatened, or attacked *him*. He may say he was trying to protect her and prevent her from hurting herself, him, or the kids.

The victim knows that if the abuser is the "golden boy" of the department or if the department has already invested a substantial amount of time and money in the abuser's training, they are likely to give him every benefit of the doubt. Though the standard of judgment in internal investigations is supposed to be a "preponderance of the evidence," in reality the standard often used is "beyond a reasonable doubt." Unless the victim has irrefutable evidence, the investigator is likely to conclude that the incident did not occur the way the victim reported it, or that she is to blame for the male officer's violence.

> *Nothing happens to him. He even got promoted and life goes on for him. Me? I don't want to get into another relationship for a long time, if ever. My life's a mess. My career's a mess. I'm in debt up to here. And I'm still*

> afraid he's going to come after me and anybody I get involved with.

On the other hand, if the department has previously identified him as a "problem officer" who is a liability risk to the agency, they are likely to use her accusation to relieve the department of that risk. The department may instruct the investigator to interrogate the victim to get the truth, even though the victim's safety may be at stake if she discloses information. The investigator may be sympathetic to the victim's situation, but nevertheless is obligated to do his or her job. The victim knows how things work and her decision to come forward implied that she was willing to deal with the consequences.

When the victim tells the investigators that she is afraid and that she believes she is in danger, the investigator might say she is exaggerating or paranoid, and minimize the abuse by saying, "He's just letting off steam, he would never hurt you," thereby undermining her perception of reality. The investigators may dismiss, minimize or discount things that are very significant from the victim's point of view, offering reckless and false assurances. She may also be reminded that she knew the procedures and should have anticipated the department's actions.

Unlike with a civilian victim, the department can order a victim who is an officer to cooperate with the investigation. Ironically, forcing the victim to divulge certain information can actually protect the abuser from criminal prosecution. If the investigator elicits information about a serious incident, and then orders the alleged abuser to answer questions regarding the incident, his compelled statement is protected under "Garrity"—the Supreme Court ruling in Garrity v. New Jersey 385 U.S. 439 (1967). "By invoking the Garrity Rights, an officer is invoking his or her right against self-incrimination. Any statements made after invoking Garrity, may only be used for departmental investigation purposes and not for criminal prosecution."[104] The department is also severely limited to only asking questions that are specific to the officer's job. "As a result, criminal prosecution of officers is more difficult. Once an officer's statement is compelled, the officer is effectively shielded from prosecution on the basis of that statement. If applied in good faith, this Supreme Court ruling would often require a trade-off between purging bad officers through administrative means versus criminal prosecution. In practice, compelled statements tend to protect officers from any sanctions, since criminal prosecution is unlikely and administrative disciplinary sanctions are applied inconsistently if at all."[105]

The formal or informal recommendation to the victim may be that she terminate the relationship to avoid future incidents or allegations that could endanger her career. This recommendation reveals ignorance of the fact that violence often escalates after separation. Nearly 90% of intimate partner homicides by men have been shown to involve a documented history of domestic violence, and a majority of these killings take place during or following separation."[106]

> [Seventy-four] percent of all murder-suicides involved an intimate partner. Of these, 96 percent were females killed by their intimate partners... This type of murder-suicide typically involves a man between the ages of 18 and 60 years old who develops suspicions of his girlfriend's or wife's infidelity, becomes enraged, murders her, and then commits suicide—usually using a firearm. Often, he will also kill the children of himself and the intimate partner.[107] Studies that compare suicide rates show that law enforcement suicide rates exceed rates for both the general

population and age/gender matched groups. No studies deal specifically with police officers involved in murder-suicide, but one reason for the higher rates cited above for law enforcement may be the easy accessibility to firearms. Experts note that the nature of police work—control over and responsibility for others—along with easy access to firearms probably plays a role in their heightened risk for murder-suicide.[108]

> *I stayed because I was terrified of the violence. He kept telling me that he'd kill me and himself, and he would have. I was his hostage. I did whatever he told me to do, I was petrified. He dry-fired his handgun when he was drinking. Oh, I forgot to tell you. He was the chief hostage negotiator.*

If the victim leaves the abuser before he is ready to let her go, or if he has threatened to kill her if she even tries to end the relationship, obviously leaving may not be her safest option. If she leaves the abuser before *she* is ready, he will exploit her ambivalence and will likely be able to manipulate her into seeing him, calling him, or having sex with him. He will then use their having been together to further prove to the department that she is not afraid of him now and never was; the allegations were false.

The chief is ultimately responsible for protecting the interest of the agency, and may have to answer to the mayor, city manager and taxpayers. The chief's obligation to protect the department and the public must override potential consequences to the victim. If the department sustains the complaint, the abuser will be disciplined or terminated. If the department does not sustain the complaint, the finding validates his prediction that he'd get away with it, increasing his power and diminishing hers.

> *A chief's view: If surrounding agencies become aware of the domestic violence, they start to ask, "Why aren't you able to keep control of your troops?" It's seen as a disgrace or black mark to the chief and agency.*

Many female officers who have reported say that if they had to do it over again, they would avoid reporting despite all costs to their personal well-being and safety. They say it was not worth the emotional trauma and embarrassment. They testify that fellow officers and supervisors punished them by ostracizing and shunning. They were harassed, radio calls interfered with, assignments were changed, they were transferred, backup failed to be provided. Such retaliation takes a tremendous emotional toll and may break a victim's spirit and determination to stand by her complaint. Some victims recant, others choose to leave the profession rather than endure the hostility and harassment. No matter what the outcome of her complaint, having made the complaint does extensive damage to her career, reputation, and her relationships within the department.

> *All of this treatment pales in comparison to how I was treated after I reported the harassment. I became a nuisance and an outcast. I received two punitive transfers when I spoke out.*

Unfortunately, the very systems that are established to investigate officer misconduct have the potential to be misused as tools to harass or retaliate against employees. Being the subject of an internal investigation can have a very serious effect on an officer's career, affecting transfers, promotions, and other benefits. The process of the investigation often causes stress to all involved parties, especially if the investigation is drawn out over a long period of time. The outcome may result in discipline and, even if there is no actual discipline, the fact of the investigation may remain on the officer's record for a period of time, possibly affecting transfers, promotions, and the officer's reputation. Women officers have reported that when they file complaints of discrimination or harassment, they subsequently become targets of internal investigations based on complaints that were often anonymous and false.[109]

> *My personal professional reputation has greatly suffered. I was on the promotional fast track until this. Rumor mongers portrayed me as a "vindictive bitch." Awful! I am doing all that I can to rebuild both [my personal and professional reputations]. I only have five and a half years until retirement. It may take all that time to achieve this.*

Reporting harassment and discrimination does not exist in a vacuum. The incidents of previous harassment and discrimination in this department become part of an oral history that every woman becomes aware of. Victims have either separated from the Department, or continued with their employment. In instances where the victim has separated from the Department, the victim has sacrificed a career which required an unparalleled level of commitment, as well as all the benefits gleaned from their career… financial, medical, retirement security. The women who have remained with the Department do not thrive. In effect, their careers were also sacrificed, with aspirations of advancement crushed. The effects of the discrimination and harassment linger long after the actual events.[110]

> The decision not to investigate and not to prosecute your friends is frequently more important than going after your enemies.[111]

Though departments defend the integrity of their investigations when "policing their own," many in and outside of the profession question whether this is an honest assessment. If an incident has come to the attention of the public, public pressure may force the department to avoid the appearance of impropriety and refer the case to the state's attorney. But, the police and the state's attorney are intertwined within the network of power, and the police can exert a great deal of pressure on the state's attorney to pursue or to not pursue criminal charges.

The political climate, public sentiment, and the department's interest in a particular case may influence the prosecutor's decision. Cases involving police officers are a tough call for the prosecutor because of the close day-to-day working relationship between the police and the prosecutor's office. The prosecutor depends on police cooperation in virtually every case that goes through the courtroom. Consequently, the prosecution of a police officer is extremely rare; winning a case against an officer without the cooperation of his employing agency is nearly impossible. "Local prosecutors work closely with police departments and, therefore, are reluctant to file criminal charges against these departments' officers."[112]

Because of the political implications involved, the prosecutor has to take care to avoid the appearance of impropriety on the part of the state. An effective way to do this is to allow the grand jury to decide. The prosecutor can do this with confidence that the grand jury will provide the desired outcome because the grand jury follows the prosecutor's recommendation the vast majority of the time. In *Above the Law: Secret Deals, Political Fixes, and Other Misadventures of the U.S. Department of Justice* David Burnham states, "Although the institution of the grand jury was originally established as a citizen check on abusive prosecutors, grand juries today almost always act as rubber stamps."[113]

The political pressure to pursue or not to pursue criminal charges may influence how the prosecutor views the evidence and whether the prosecutor finds the victim to be a credible witness for the state. If the prosecutor is not convinced that it is a winnable case, the prosecutor will not proceed with the charges. If there is public pressure to "do *something*" the prosecutor may charge the officer but then offer him an opportunity to plead to a lesser charge that will not affect his ability to carry a weapon.

> Prosecutors use the theoretical independence of the grand jury to escape public criticism when, for one reason or another, the prosecutor decides not to bring charges in a particularly notorious case. It is not uncommon… for a prosecutor confronted with pressures from the news media to shift the burden for declining prosecution to the grand jury. In this way he avoids any personal accountability for the ultimate decision.[114]

The courts and/or prosecutors tend to see a case as "not winnable" because a jury would never believe a cop would do that. So, the case never gets charged.

My family law attorney kept saying, "We don't want to risk him losing his job, you may end up paying spousal

> *support if that happens. Believe me, things will be much worse if he gets fired."*

All police officers know how the system works—that the truth and the facts in a case are subject to the interpretation and manipulation of many people and can easily lose their connection to reality. Both the accused officer and the victim know that in criminal court, what matters is not what actually took place but what the state is able—beyond a reasonable doubt—to prove took place.

> *One of his favorite taunts was, "You got pictures? If not then it didn't happen." He knew it would be my word against his, and his word had more credibility.*

The word of officers is accepted as true in police reports and in court testimony when they are acting in their official capacity. But when the female officer gives sworn testimony about her own personal experience her credibility, her honesty, her perceptions and her recollection of the incident are judged to be less credible and carry less weight in most courtrooms than that of the defendant or the male officers who testify in court.

The female officer, like every other woman, faces the presumption that women lie about domestic violence and sexual assault. "There is a bias against women in the court," former United States Justice

> Though women have greater protections today, they have long been the victims of prejudice and bias at the hands of law enforcement officials.[115] Women continue to be murdered, mugged, assaulted, battered, and raped in the United States. And it is not always clear that laws, law enforcement officials, or the legal system deter, prevent, or have the will to prosecute the men carrying out the crimes.[116]

Department official Bonnie Campbell said in an interview in 2001. "Most players in the courtroom are men, and one of their greatest fears is that they will be falsely accused of rape. The question 'Is she telling the truth?' inserts itself into every case."[117]

Should the victim decide that the state's victory in winning a conviction or "cleaning up the police department" are not worth the risk to her personal safety or her career, she is in a "double double-bind." The prosecutor may proceed without her testimony or force her to testify, jeopardizing her safety and her career. Her options are to testify honestly or change her story and risk being charged with perjury. The prosecutor who proceeds is likely to do so zealously. The prosecutor may be motivated by the desire to demonstrate that the state has the power to hold the police accountable, and to send a message to the community that police officers are not above the law. And, the department may cooperate, seizing the opportunity to demonstrate to the public that the department is genuinely committed to holding abusive officers accountable.

If she recants, she permanently damages her credibility. The state's attorney may use her case as an example when explaining why the state routinely screens out domestic violence complaints against officers. The state's attorney uses her recantation as verification that women commonly make false allegations.

Neither the prosecutor nor the department can protect the victim, yet they can demand that she participate in the process. Ultimately, they believe, as does the abuser, that she got herself into the whole mess: she was in a relationship with him, she decided to report to the police, she made a statement, and she provided evidence. She is a cop and she knows how the criminal justice system works; she has to accept the consequences.

Advocates in the Network

"'Twenty-five years ago we had a notion that we were organizing to change the system,' says Ellen Pence... 'Then this funny change happened, where instead of us advocating for what women needed from the system, we started advocating the system to women. There has to be a new confrontation of what's going on.'"[118] A female officer may not consider domestic violence counseling, advocacy programs, or shelters viable options. There are many reasons for this, including embarrassment that she, a cop, is a victim. She fears that advocates and other victims would lose confidence in her ability to protect them. She may be worried about the repercussions of violating the rule that "what happens in the department stays in the department," or she may not want to taint the public's image of the police. She may not want to endanger other victims, counselors, or shelter staff should the abuser follow her.

> *I didn't file a lawsuit with the department, and I'm glad I didn't because I was a Detective on domestic violence cases. It could have hurt the victims on my cases because the department would think I was biased.*

In the beginning of the Battered Women's Movement, advocates and police departments were more likely than not to be adversaries. This has changed dramatically over the years as government funding has required police and advocates to work together. In the beginning, advocates kept the location of their programs and shelters as secret as possible from everyone, including the police. Today, police officers routinely transport victims to the shelters. Advocates had victims sign confidentiality agreements before they discussed anything with the advocate. Today, it is as likely that they have the woman sign a release of information so that the "case" can be discussed among the members of the network. In some communities, the network of power has co-opted community-based advocates. There are areas of the country where the *only* victim services are incorporated into the police department or prosecutor's office.

Cooperation between advocates and police can be beneficial to both parties and to many civilian victims, but it presents complex problems when the alleged perpetrator or victim is a police officer. It is becoming more common for police officers or chiefs to be members of domestic violence agencies' boards of directors. This gives the police an opportunity to influence domestic violence agency policy and procedures; a situation involving an officer can obviously present conflicts of interest.

Sadly, many female officers don't seek assistance from domestic violence advocates because they don't trust them. They fear that the advocates' allegiance to or fear of the police they work with will prove to be stronger than their ability or willingness to assist her. They are aware that the advocates know the abuser; all too often he is on the domestic violence response unit. He may be the one the advocates and victims see as the "knight in shining armor," the sensitive cop who gets it. He appears to have respect for the women officers he works with, for the advocates and for victims. The advocates and the victims feel comfortable with him, confide in him and trust him to protect them from violent men—and from the less sensitive cops in the department. The female officer whose abuser is the favorite of the advocate community is not likely to look to the advocates for help.

Whether the victim is local or from another state, she knows that advocates may be ambivalent about getting involved. Granted, there are legitimate security concerns for all involved if the abuser is able to find or has access to the shelter. Unfortunately, sometimes the real reason is that the program fears the political repercussions of getting involved with a police case. They feel they cannot afford to jeopardize their friendly relationship with the police because of funding considerations, their reputation in the community, or their ability to assist civilian victims if they incur the wrath of the police department.

> *I don't believe the victim advocacy tree is safe for female officers. Based on my experience, it is used against female officer-victims. Trying to survive on your own without these system-funded groups is much healthier. It isn't about the victims at all, it's only about the arm-wrestling to secure funding.*

> *At first, I was not offered a victim advocate. Fourteen months after I first reported, the department realized that it was part of their policy to hook me up with an advocate. They appointed a prosecutor-based advocate. I left her multiple voice mails, she never once called back, but she did forward my voice mails to "the enemy"—the attorney for the Sheriff's Department.*

The abuser who works with the advocates can manipulate their personal and professional relationships to gain their sympathy the same way he does with fellow officers. He can set the stage by telling the advocates that he and his intimate partner have been having problems and warn them that she might contact them. He says she is trying to get him into trouble with the department. He paints her as controlling, vindictive, violent, or unstable. He tells the advocates that his understanding and sympathy towards victims is a result of his own victimization; he "knows how it feels." By claiming to be the victim, the abuser can even receive advocacy services from the agency. This, of course, blocks access to services for his victim.

It is not unusual for an officer who has been accused of abusing his intimate partner to get romantically involved with an advocate. He uses his relationship with the advocate to show that a woman who is knowledgeable about domestic violence sees him as a nice guy and feels safe dating him. This helps remove any doubts others may have that it is his ex— not he—who is the problem. This strategy is also effective in increasing the victim's isolation.

The community-based advocate's role should be distinguishable from that of the victim witness liaison's role in that the advocate's job is to advocate for the victim's requests, not to facilitate the agenda of the police department or the prosecutor's office. The advocate's purpose is to confront and fight the system on the *victim's* behalf, as opposed to working with the victim on the *system's* behalf. Those who are employed by the system are limited in their capacity to monitor the system.

Some police agencies frown upon an officer using community-based advocacy services. The department risks losing control of the situation if an outside advocate is involved. The advocate may give the victim information that the department would prefer she does not have. Conversely, the victim may give the advocate information about the abuser and operations that the department does not want the advocate to have. The involvement of an outsider threatens exposure of the department, intruding upon the privacy of the police family. Should the victim give the advocate permission, the advocate could share this information with the community, city officials and the media. Advocates can further pressure the prosecutor to pursue criminal charges against an officer.

In some ways, however, having an advocate involved can benefit the department. For example, if the department would prefer to remain ignorant of a situation, the victim can get information and talk about her options with someone outside the department who is not mandated to report internally. Once there is a 911 call and an official report, however, the police may interpret the advocate's involvement as intrusive and as "interfering with an investigation."

There are conflicts of interest among the various players in the system when the victim or perpetrator is an officer. Some are invested in covering-up the incident, others may be equally invested in exposing it. Advocates can get caught in the cross-fire. Like prosecutors and other players, advocates need the cooperation of the local police in much of their work. The battered women in the community rely on the police for protection; an adversarial relationship between the police and the advocates can affect police response for all victims. Though advocates do not want officers who batter to respond to domestic violence calls in the community, they are reluctant to alienate the local police.

Community agencies and the department may view the establishment of a collaborative working relationship as a way to access information from each other, thereby increasing their respective power. This might work if the relationship were egalitarian, but it is not. The department has power over the community agency. Nowhere does this become more obvious than in a case involving a police officer. Though the department "allows" advocates to respond to domestic violence scenes, access police reports and be privy to other details of an investigation, the permission can be withdrawn at any time, cutting advocates out of the loop. Department liaisons employ the guise of being forbidden to talk about an ongoing investigation, or they simply tell the advocates that the department is handling the situation internally and that the police are not required to answer to the advocates for the department's internal operations.

If the department wants information about the victim or the situation from the advocate, however, they can demand the information, sometimes going so far as to subpoena advocates' records. There have been situations in which the police have accused advocates of aiding and abetting a fugitive, or concealing evidence when advocates have refused to give them information about a police victim. The collaborative relationship quickly turns adversarial, the illusion of being a "team" shatters.

Advocates try to avoid these conflicts because of the damage the police can do to their reputation, funding, community relationships and the overall safety of battered women. At the same time, advocates cannot turn their backs on victims of abusive police officers, whether the victim is a civilian or an officer. When the police are able to include advocates in their network of power and align advocates with the department against the most vulnerable victims—those who are police officers—they have successfully negated the meaning of the word "advocate."

Crossing the Threshold

> One genius of the system we live under is that the strategies it requires to survive it from day to day are exactly the opposite of what is required to change it.[119]

At some point, the chief or department spokesperson may have to address the public regarding a case that has made the news. Their approach varies in accordance with the circumstances. If the public knows that there were previous allegations against the offending officer, the chief may say that there was not enough evidence to sustain the complaint or pursue criminal charges. The department only had a "he said, she said" situation. If a previous complaint was sustained, the chief will say that the department handled it appropriately in-house. If the case was

> Most states have adopted laws intended to protect police officers and other civil servants from arbitrary or politically motivated reprisal. In practice, though, these measures also severely restrict the authority of a police chief to discipline abusive officers. Even in cases where department officials have dismissed officers for repeated acts of brutality, the officers have sometimes won reinstatement through legal appeals or the arbitration process.[120]

prosecuted and the officer was acquitted, he will say that the department was justified in not taking further action.

In other circumstances, the chief will claim that the department had no knowledge of the abuse. No one on the department knew anything because if they had, they'd have been duty-bound to report any misconduct. The chief asserts that "there was just no way they could have seen this coming," and denies that there were any warning signs. The chief speculates that the officer must have just "snapped," perhaps as a result of the pressures of the job, depression, exhaustion, burnout, indulgence in alcohol or drugs, or relationship problems that sparked uncontrollable anger or jealousy. The speculation that the officer's behavior was caused by any of these "maladies" may solicit questions about the officer's fitness for duty. The chief is walking a fine line: it must be clear that no one saw any indications that the officer's personal problems were affecting his job performance and it was an "isolated incident."

> *The early warning systems often ignore significant flags by "silo-ing": viewing one event as it stands alone. If all the events, citizen complaints and internal complaints were reviewed cumulatively, patterns would become evident. Silo-ing enables agency heads to articulate compliance with the early warning system standards.*

Warning signs of intimate partner abuse *are* difficult, if not impossible, to identify in a hypermasculine culture where "normal" behavior is very similar or identical to the behavior of a batterer. If the particular department's culture allows or encourages aggressive, intimidating, misogynistic behavior, abusive behavior will simply blend in.

> *I think that many cops demonstrate or share flags or indicators of abuse with their peers. It isn't as common*

> to hear actual admissions of assault on a domestic partner as it is to hear admissions of consistent excessive use of force on "customers" being dealt with on the street as if it were something to be proud of, the mark of strength and control over the "lesser good."

Some chiefs say that the department doesn't have the authority to control off-duty behavior. This is another fine line, because the department actually *does* regulate many types of off-duty behavior and activities. Professional ethics do extend to officers' personal lives. Yet, when it comes to domestic violence, it is evident that the use of the power *not* to exercise authority is as significant as the use of power *to* exercise authority. We must question why violence against an intimate partner is where they choose to not cross the line into an officer's private life.

Police believe that "the best predictor of future behavior is past behavior." This is why they check a suspect's record. They also know certain entries can look bad on an officer's record without further explanation or statement of outcome. To ensure that past allegations do not haunt officers throughout their careers, many collective bargaining agreements mandate that an officer's personnel jacket is periodically purged of all unsustained complaints. Unfortunately, this prevents IA from being able to identify a pattern of complaints against a specific officer. This is particularly problematic in respect to domestic violence, sexual assault and rape because such allegations are rarely sustained. A sporadic history of complaints over several years could reveal a pattern, but when the file is purged, the officer gets a fresh start. Knowing that an officer with a reputation for aggression and assault against women is periodically "absolved of his sins" adds to the sense of powerlessness and futility for female officers who consider reporting abuse.

The media is the department's conduit for community relations and information. Public information officers control the story that is released. Many reporters are enmeshed in the network of power because the police and the prosecutor are their sources of information. After an incident involving an officer, the media dutifully reports that there was no way the department could have seen it coming. The officer was by all accounts a "good man and a good cop." Friends, neighbors, fellow officers and supervisors vouch for the officer's character. Something or someone must have made him snap. The story may include subtle victim-blaming language or incidents from the victim's past that cast a shadow of doubt on her character or credibility—even though she, too, is a police officer. There is often a statement or insinuation that help would have been readily available had the victim simply reported the abuse.

If case facts reveal that the offender was not a good man and a good cop but was, in fact, a volatile man and a brutal cop, the department assures the public that this officer is an anomaly. His behavior in no way reflects the standards of the department. He is an embarrassment to the department. It would be unfair of the public to judge other officers based on his aberrant behavior.

> A scandal breaks and the chief trots out the favored litany, "The vast majority of our cops are honest, dedicated public servants. These guys… are just a few rotten apples in an otherwise healthy barrel." The overwhelming majority of cops are dedicated, noble workers, but the unstated truth is that they are all complicit in the code of silence.[121] [They] are content to live in uneasy symbiosis with the rotten.[122]

The chief must be sure that the media conveys the message that the department takes police-perpetrated domestic violence very seriously. He tells the public that his strong and clear message to the officers is zero tolerance for domestic violence. The department has (or will soon have) a specific policy on officer-involved domestic violence and specific (re-)training to address the issue. The chief must have the public's confidence in his ability to lead.

Talking in terms of policy is an effective public relations strategy, but it should not misdirect the public's focus—or that of the department. Policy *can* improve response, and training officers *is* essential, but training can be conducted in such a way as to fail to challenge attitudes and behaviors, and policy can be ignored by the culture.

Once out of the spotlight, the chief warns the officers that domestic violence will not be tolerated. They should not be stupid—only an idiot would jeopardize his career by using violence against an intimate partner. Women in departments with a dominant sexist and masculine culture say that the men interpret this warning as, "You know where the line is, don't cross it." A local chief said he explains it to his men this way, "You can always get another woman, you can't always get another career."

The smart cop uses every tactic of control and coercion short of physical abuse. Like on the job, he is capable of gaining and maintaining control without the use of physical force. Manipulation, isolation, intimidation, interrogation, degradation, humiliation and coercion—especially a combination of them in the context of inescapable confinement—are more than enough to produce the desired outcome of compliance and control. The beauty of these tactics is that they are not illegal and they leave no physical evidence. He asks the victim, "What are you going to tell them, that I hurt your feelings?"

Men complain that the definition of domestic violence and abusive behavior is so broad that it covers just about all male behavior. The fact that abusive behavior doesn't stand out as abusive should be a warning sign in itself. Men reassure women they're not like other men, male officers reassure women that they're not like other cops, they're safe to be with, they won't harm her. *What is wrong with this picture?*

What is wrong is that "normal" male behavior often is indistinguishable from abusive behavior. Lip service isn't enough. Going through the motions isn't enough. Attitudes and beliefs seep through. The goal is not just to make it *appear* that police officers get it. The goal is to make them *actually* get it.

As long as the preservation of male power is the highest value of our culture—both in the general culture and the police culture—men will continue to use force to maintain their power. Those who profess a desire to end violence against women while still maintaining the present social order are caught in a conundrum. Society may evolve to the point where male violence is rarely physical, but men will always retain the threat and capacity to use it.

Law enforcement is the only institution that has the authority to use force to control others. Since they are the last bastion of male power and authority, the public should be paying attention to the way male police officers treat female officers both on the job and in their intimate relationships. Robin Morgan says that "women are the canaries in the mine…" The way the police culture treats female officers gives us tremendous insight into how it views all women and all "others." It tells us everything about the dynamics of social justice and the preservation of male power.

We see the results of male violence. Police violence against women isn't contained in the police agencies or in their homes. It spills over on all of us. Police-perpetrated domestic violence is perhaps the most insidious form of police brutality.

Citizens foot the bill. We pay for the selection, hiring and training of police officers. We pay for their equipment, their salaries, their benefits and their retirement. We pay for the defense of lawsuits and we pay the settlement costs of the lawsuits—millions of dollars a year in many cities. The costs in terms of social justice are incalculable. As it stands today, anyone who is not white, male, affluent and heterosexual is a potential victim of police brutality.

> The average male officer on a big city police agency costs taxpayers somewhere between two-and-a-half and five-and-a-half times more than the average woman officer in excessive force liability lawsuit payouts. He is also eight and a half times more likely to have an allegation of excessive force sustained against him, and he is two to three times more likely to have a citizen name him in a complaint of excessive force.[123]

It isn't just the good police officers who stand by and do nothing. We *all* collude when, as good citizens, we stand by and do nothing. Whose responsibility is it to change the culture? The presence of female officers influences the police culture, but they cannot change it without a tremendous shift in society's attitudes towards women and others. We need to wake up and break through our denial because society cannot afford to lose the women who work in the criminal justice system. Ask any female victim of violence—on the streets or in the homes of America—what kind of response does she receive from the male-dominated criminal justice system? What would happen to victims of domestic violence, sexual assault and rape if policing was left entirely in the hands of men whose only value is the protection of their own power?

Female officers are leaving the profession because of men's attitude towards them, the network of power from which they are excluded, and because they are victims of assault and battery perpetrated by male officers—even in their own homes. We will not stop violence against women as long as we refuse to challenge men's sense of entitlement to do as they please in their own homes. We find ourselves in a vicious circle that starts and ends with law enforcement. We have to cross the thresholds of their homes.

> A corrupt, racist, or brutal cop will abstain from misconduct only when he looks at the cop next to him and believes that the officer will blow the whistle… Real reform is possible only when that value system changes and cops come to realize that they must police themselves.[124]

What will it take to make them hear?

It's said that women are society's canaries in the mine—living alerts to danger—and it's true that a civilization can be gauged by the status of its female citizens. But miners pay *attention* to the canaries' health and reactions, since they know that this information is crucial to their own survival. So far—35 years into the current feminist wave, and despite remarkable gains won—warnings from female human beings still are not heeded sufficiently, and most male human beings still don't understand that their own lives depend on that heeding.[125]

In Honor of Those Silenced

To our sisters who remain unnamed or
unknown,
the living and dead and missing...
To those who have lost their lives
and
to those living
who have lost their spirits,
their careers, their families, their children
and their homes...

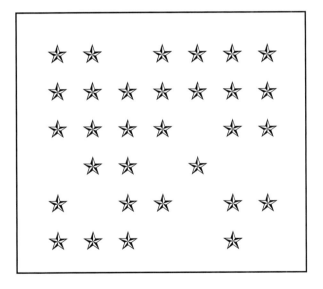

References

Aaron, Susan. "Women with Badges." <http://featuredreports.monster.com/law_enforcement/women/>.

Austin, Wendy. "The Socialisation of Women: Male Police Officer Hostility to Female Police Officers." (Paper presented at the Australian Institute of Criminology Conference, First Australasian Women Police Conference. Sydney, Australia, 29–31 July 1996.)

Bancroft, Lundy and Jay Silverman. *The Batterer as Parent: Addressing the Impact of Domestic Violence on Family Dynamics*. Thousand Oaks, CA: Sage Publications, 2002.

Barker, Thomas and David L. Carter. *Police Deviance*, 3rd ed. Cincinnati: Anderson Publishing, 1994.

Bergen, G. Terry, Christine Bourne-Lindamood and Sarah Brecknock. "Incidence of Domestic Violence Among Rural and Small Town Law Enforcement Officers." In *Domestic Violence by Police Officers*, ed. D.C. Sheehan, 63–73. Washington, DC: U.S. Department of Justice, 2000.

Bolton, Kenneth Jr. and Joe R. Feagin. *Black in Blue: African-American Police Officers and Racism*. New York: Routledge, 2004.

Boulin Johnson, Leanor. "Burnout and Work and Family Violence Among Police: Gender Comparisons." In *Domestic Violence by Police Officers*, ed. D.C. Sheehan, 107–121. Washington, DC: U.S. Department of Justice, 2000.

Boulin Johnson, Leanor, Michael Todd and Ganga Subramanian. "Violence in Police Families: Work-Violence Spillover." *Journal of Family Violence*, 20 (2005): 3–12.

Bouza, Anthony V. *The Police Mystique: An Insider's Look at Cops, Crime, and the Criminal Justice System*. New York: Plenum Press, 1990.

Bouza, Anthony V. *Police Unbound: Corruption, Abuse, and Heroism by the Boys in Blue*. New York: Prometheus Books, 2001.

Bovard, James. "The Latest Gun Control Fiasco." <http://www.fff.org/freedom/0597d.asp>.

Bureau of Justice Statistics. *Law Enforcement Management and Administrative Statistics: Local Police Departments, 2003*. Washington, DC: U.S. Department of Justice, 2006.

Burk, Martha. *The Cult of Power: Sex Discrimination in Corporate America and What Can Be Done About It.* New York: A Lisa Drew Book/Scribner, 2005.

Burnham, David. *Above the Law: Secret Deals, Political Fixes, and Other Misadventures of the U.S. Department of Justice.* New York: Scribner, 1996.

Buzawa, Eve S. and Carl G. Buzawa. "Traditional and Innovative Police Responses to Domestic Violence." In *Critical Issues in Policing: Contemporary Readings,* 4th ed., eds. Roger G. Dunham & Geoffrey P. Alpert, 216–237. Prospect Heights, IL: Waveland Press, 2001.

Campbell, Jacquelyn C. (ed.) *Assessing Dangerousness: Violence by Sex Offenders, Batterers and Child Abusers.* London: Sage Publications, 1996.

Campion, Michale A. "Small Police Departments and Police Officer-Involved Domestic Violence: A Survey in Domestic Violence by Police Officers." In *Domestic Violence by Police Officers*, ed. D.C. Sheehan, 123–131. Washington, DC: U.S. Department of Justice, 2000.

Cash, Rosanne and Rodney Crowell. "Real Woman" in *Interiors,* Columbia/Legacy compact disc 82876776382, 1990.

Catania, Sara. "The Counselor." *Mother Jones,* 30 (2005): 44-49, 88.

Chesler, Phyllis. *Mothers on Trial: The Battle for Children & Custody.* New York: McGraw-Hill Book Co., 1986.

Cothran, Helen, ed. *Police Brutality: Current Controversies.* San Diego: Greenhaven Press, 2004.

Crank, John P. *Understanding Police Culture.* Cincinnati: Anderson Publishing Co., 1998.

Delattre, Edwin J. *Character and Cops: Ethics in Policing.* Washington, DC: American Enterprise Institute for Public Policy Research, 2002.

Department of Public Safety, City of Indianapolis, Indianapolis Police Department. "*History: Women and Minorities.*" <http://www.indygov.org/eGov/City/DPS/IPD/About/History/home.htm>.

Dulaney, W. Marvin. *Black Police in America.* Bloomington, IN: Indiana University Press, 1996.

Dunham, Roger G. and Geoffrey P. Alpert, eds. *Critical Issues in Policing: Contemporary Readings* 4th ed. Prospect Heights, IL: Waveland Press, 2001.

Enloe, Cynthia. *Maneuvers: The International Politics of Militarizing Women's Lives*. Berkeley: University of California Press, 2000.

Family Violence Prevention Fund. "Domestic Violence Is a Serious, Widespread Social Problem in America: The Facts." <http://www.endabuse.org/resources/facts/>.

Feagin, Joe R. and Hernán Vera. *White Racism: The Basics*. New York: Routledge, 1995.

Federal Law Enforcement Training Center. "Sexual Discrimination and Sexual Harassment in the Workplace: A Legal Overview." <http://www.fletc.gov/legal/platp/TitleVIIsex.doc>.

Ferrara, Lauren and Robin Smith. "Lawsuit filed March 23, 2005 by Lauren Ferrara and Robin Smith v. County of Sonoma Sheriff's Department." <http://www.justicewomen.com/complaint_real.pdf>.

Fletcher, Connie. *Breaking and Entering: Women Cops Talk About Life in the Ultimate Men's Club*. New York: HarperCollins Publishers, 1995.

Florida Law Enforcement and Police News. "The Garrity Warning." <www.flacops.com/Garrity-Warning.htm>.

Florida State University Office of Research. "Research in Review: Slavery's Police." <http://www.research.fsu.edu/researchr/issue2001/slavery.html>.

Frye, Marilyn. *Politics of Reality: Essays in Feminist Theory*. Freedom, CA: The Crossing Press, 1983.

Fyfe, James J., Jack R. Greene, William F. Walsh, O. W. Wilson and Roy C. McLaren. *Police Administration*, 5th ed. New York: McGraw-Hill, 1997.

Gale, Mary Ellen. "Calling in the Girl Scouts: Feminist Legal Theory and Police Misconduct." *Loyola of Los Angeles Law Review*, 34 (2001): 691-747.

Gerdes, Louise I., ed. *Police Brutality: Current Controversies*. San Diego: Greenhaven Press, 2004.

Gombossy, George. "Torrington Suit Held Valid Wives May Sue Police for Protection." *The Hartford Courant,* Oct. 24, 1984. <http://www.jud.state.ct.us/publications/Curriculum/Curriculum7.pdf>.

Gun Control Act of 1968, 18 U.S.C. § 925 (1996).

Harrington, Penny. "Civil Rights Testimony of Chief Penny Harrington, United States Commission on Civil Rights." (Public hearing panel on Racial and Ethnic Tensions in American Communities: Poverty, Inequality and Discrimination in Los

Angeles, California, Sept. 12, 1996.) <http://www.pennyharrington.com/civilrightspenny1.htm>.

Harrington, Penny. *Triumph of Spirit*. Chicago: Britanny Publications, 1999.

Holmstrom, David. "Women Officers Arrest the Gender Gap." *The Christian Science Monitor*, Jan. 12, 2000. <http://www.csmonitor.com/atcsmonitor/specials/women/work/work011200.html>.

Human Rights Watch. *Shielded from Justice: Police Brutality and Accountability in the United States*. New York: Human Rights Watch, 1998.

Hutzel, Eleanor. "The Policewoman." *The Annals – November 1929*. <http://www.sameshield.com/press/sspress119.html>.

International Association of Chiefs of Police. "Discussion Paper on IACP's Policy on Domestic Violence by Police Officers." <http://www.theiacp.org/documents/pdfs/Publications/domviolconceptpaper.pdf>.

Irving, Lesley. "Abused Women – Experiences of the Criminal Justice System." <http://www.changeweb.org.uk/abused_women.htm>.

Jones, Ann. *Next Time She'll Be Dead: Battering and How to Stop It*. New York: Beacon Press, 1994.

Jones-Brown, Delores D. *Race, Crime, and Punishment*. Philadelphia: Chelsea House Publishers, 2000.

Kappeler, Victor. "Kentucky's Response to the Lautenberg Act: Curbing Domestic Violence Among Police." <http://www.lawenforcement.eku.edu/Kjsrb/FEBRUARY99.html>.

Kappeler, Victor, Richard D. Sluder and Geoffrey P. Alpert. *Forces of Deviance: Understanding the Dark Side of Policing*. Prospect Heights, IL: Waveland Press, 1994.

Kappeler, Victor, Richard D. Sluder and Geoffrey P. Alpert. "Breeding Deviant Conformity." In *Critical Issues in Policing: Contemporary Readings*, 4th ed, eds. Roger G. Dunham and Geoffrey P. Alpert, 290–316. Prospect Heights, IL: Waveland Press, 2001.

Kiernan, Kathleen. "Public Management 1942." *Women Police in Cities*. <http://www.sameshield.com/press/sspress103.html>.

Klein, Robin and Constance Klein. "The Extent of Domestic Violence Within Law Enforcement: An Empirical Study." In *Domestic Violence by Police Officers*, ed. D.C. Sheehan, 225–232. Washington, DC: U.S. Department of Justice, 2000.

"LAPD Working to Get More Female Police Officers." *Los Angeles Times,* May 30, 2003. <http://www.sameshield.com/news/lapd.html>.

Lonsway, Kimberly, Margaret Moore, Penny Harrington, et al. "A Content Analysis of Civil Liability Cases, Sustained Allegations and Citizen Complaints." <http://www.pennyharrington.com/excessiveforceanaly.htm>.

Lonsway, Kimberly, Margaret Moore, Penny Harrington, et al. "Hiring & Retaining More Women: The Advantages to Law Enforcement Agencies." <http://www.womenandpolicing.org/pdf/NewAdvantagesReport.pdf>.

Lonsway, Kimberly, Patricia Aguirre, Nicole Gilliams, et al. "Under Scrutiny: The Effect of Consent Decrees on the Representation of Women in Sworn Law Enforcement." Los Angeles: National Center for Women & Policing, 2003.

Lonsway, Kimberly, Diane Wetendorf and Pete Conis. "Lessons Learned from Tacoma: The Problem of Police Officer Domestic Violence." *Law Enforcement Executive Forum* 3 (2003): 27-36.

MacKinnon, Catharine A. *Feminism Unmodified: Discourses on Life and Law*. Cambridge: Harvard University Press, 1987.

Martin, Susan E. *Breaking & Entering: Police Women on Patrol*. Berkeley: University of California Press, 1980.

Martin, Susan E. "Doing Gender, Doing Police Work: An Examination of the Barriers to the Integration of Women Officers." (Paper presented at the Australian Institute of Criminology Conference, First Australasian Women Police Conference. Sydney, Australia, 29–31 July 1996.)

Martin, Susan E. and Nancy C. Jurik. *Doing Justice, Doing Gender: Women in Law and Criminal Justice Occupations*. Thousand Oaks, CA: Sage Publications, 1996.

McNamara, Joseph D. "Police Corruption Is Widespread." In *Police Brutality: Opposing Viewpoints,* ed. Helen Cothran. San Diego: Greenhaven Press, 2001.

Meyer, Ed, Kim Hone-McMahan and Keith McKnight. "Few Lose Jobs." *Akron Beacon Journal,* Dec. 5, 1999, A1.

Morgan, Robin. *The Demon Lover: The Roots of Terrorism*. New York: Washington Square Press, 2001.

Morrison, Shannon, Jennifer Hardison, Anita Mathew and Joyce O'Neil. "An Evidence-Based Review of Sexual Assault Preventive Intervention Programs." (Technical report prepared for National

Institute of Justice, 2006.) <www.ncjrs.gov/pdffiles1/nij/grants/207262.pdf>.

National Center for Women & Policing. *Recruiting and Retaining Women: A Self-Assessment Guide for Law Enforcement.* Los Angeles: Feminist Majority Foundation, 1999.

Novick, Michael. "The Media Underestimates Police Brutality." In *Police Brutality: Current Controversies,* ed. Louise I. Gerdes. San Diego: Greenhaven Press, 2004.

Puddington, Arch. "The Extent of Police Brutality Is Exaggerated." In *Police Brutality: Opposing Viewpoints,* ed. Helen Cothran. San Diego: Greenhaven Press, 2004.

Rogers, Darlene D. "Recruitment and Retention of Minorities and Women in Law Enforcement." (M.A. dissertation, State University of New York Empire State College, 2004.)

Rojek, Jeff, Allen E. Wagner and Scott H. Decker. "Addressing Police Misconduct: The Role of Citizens' Complaints." In *Critical Issues in Policing: Contemporary Readings,* 4th ed., eds. Roger G. Dunham and Geoffrey P. Alpert. Prospect Heights, IL: Waveland Press, 317–337, 2001.

Rothenberg, Paula S., Nicolaus Schafhausen and Caroline Schneider. *Race, Class & Gender in the United States: An Integrated Study,* 5th ed. New York: Worth Publishers, 2000.

Rowland, Debran. *The Boundaries of Her Body: The Troubling History of Women's Rights in America.* Naperville, IL: Sphinx Publishing, 2004.

Sheehan, Donald C., ed. *Domestic Violence by Police Officers.* Washington, DC: U.S. Department of Justice, 2000.

Skolnick, Jerome H. and James J. Fyfe. *Above the Law: Police and the Excessive Use of Force.* New York: The Free Press, 1993.

Swanson, Charles R., Leonard Territo and Robert W. Taylor. *Police Administration: Structures, Processes, and Behavior,* 5th ed. Upper Saddle River, NJ: Prentice Hall, 2001.

Tice, Karen W. *Tales of Wayward Girls and Immoral Women.* Urbana, IL: University of Illinois Press, 1998.

U.S. Dept. of Justice Bureau of Justice Statistics. "State and Local Law Enforcement Statistics." <http://www.ojp.usdoj.gov/bjs/sandlle.htm>.

Violanti, John M. A. "Partnership Against Police Domestic Violence: The Police and Health Care Systems." In *Domestic Violence by*

Police Officers, ed. D.C. Sheehan. Washington, DC: U.S. Department of Justice, 2000.

Violence Policy Center. "American Roulette: Murder-Suicide in the United States." Washington DC: Violence Policy Center, 2006. <http://www.vpc.org/studies/amroul2006.pdf>.

Walker, Samuel. *The Police in America: An Introduction,* 3rd ed. New York: McGraw-Hill, 1999.

Websdale, Neil. *Rural Woman Battering and the Justice System: An Ethnography*. Thousand Oaks, CA: Sage Publications, 1997.

Websdale, Neil. *Policing the Poor: From Slave Plantation to Public Housing*. Boston: Northeastern University Press, 2001.

Wetendorf, Diane. Interview on *National Public Radio (WBEZ). All Things Considered*, March 4, 1996.

Wetendorf, Diane. *When the Batterer Is a Law Enforcement Officer: A Guide for Advocates*. Minneapolis: Battered Women's Justice Project, 2004.

Wetendorf, Diane. *Police Domestic Violence: A Handbook for Victims*. Arlington Heights, IL: Diane Wetendorf, Inc., 2006.

Wetendorf, Diane and Dottie L. Davis. "Developing Policy on Officer-Involved Domestic Violence." In *Advocate and Officer Dialogues: Police-Perpetrated Domestic Violence,* 19–29. Arlington Heights, IL: Diane Wetendorf, Inc., 2003.

Wetendorf, Diane and Dottie L. Davis. "The Misuse of Police Powers in Officer-Involved Domestic Violence." In *Advocate and Officer Dialogues: Police-Perpetrated Domestic Violence*, 1–17. Arlington Heights, IL: Diane Wetendorf, Inc., 2004.

White, Paul. (1996). "Constraints Affecting the Career Development of Policewomen." (Paper presented at the Australian Institute of Criminology Conference, First Australasian Women Police Conference. Sydney, Australia, 29–31 July 1996.)

Women Deputies of the Sonoma County Sheriff's Department. "Letter to Sheriff Cogbill." (Dec. 22, 2004.) <http://www.justicewomen.com/cc_letter_to_department.pdf>.

Women's Justice Center. "More Sexism Than Ever at Sonoma County Sheriff's Department." <http://www.justicewomen.com/pw_law_suit.html>.

Yoshino, Kenji. *Covering: The Hidden Assault on Our Civil Rights*. New York: Random House, 2006.

Endnotes

[1] Paul White, "Constraints Affecting the Career Development of Policewomen." (Paper presented at the Australian Institute of Criminology Conference, First Australasian Women Police Conference. Sydney, Australia, 29–31 July 1996).

[2] Lauren Ferrara and Robin Smith, "Lawsuit filed March 23, 2005 by Lauren Ferrara and Robin Smith v. County of Sonoma Sheriff's Department." <http://www.justicewomen.com/complaint_real.pdf>.

[3] Bureau of Justice Statistics, *Law Enforcement Management and Administrative Statistics: Local Police Departments, 2003.* (Washington, DC: U.S. Department of Justice, 2006).

[4] Ann Jones, *Next Time She'll Be Dead: Battering and How to Stop It.* (New York: Beacon Press, 1994), 3.

[5] Samuel Walker, *The Police in America: An Introduction,* 3rd ed. (New York: McGraw-Hill, 1999), 230.

[6] Victor Kappeler, Richard D. Sluder and Geoffrey P. Alpert. "Breeding Deviant Conformity." In *Critical Issues in Policing: Contemporary Readings,* 4th ed, eds. Roger G. Dunham and Geoffrey P. Alpert. (Prospect Heights, IL: Waveland Press, 2001), 290.

[7] Kappeler, Sluder & Alpert, 295.

[8] Kenji Yoshino, *Covering: The Hidden Assault on Our Civil Rights.* (New York: Random House, 2006), x.

[9] Florida State University Office of Research, "Research in Review: Slavery's Police." <http://www.research.fsu.edu/researchr/issue2001/slavery.html>.

[10] Florida State Univ.

[11] Delores D. Jones-Brown, *Race, Crime, and Punishment.* (Philadelphia: Chelsea House Publishers, 2000), 26.

[12] W. Marvin Dulaney, *Black Police in America.* (Bloomington, IN: Indiana University Press, 1996), 55.

[13] Dulaney, 64.

[14] Dulaney, 64.

[15] Dulaney, x.

[16] Karen W. Tice, *Tales of Wayward Girls and Immoral Women.* (Urbana, IL: Univ. of Illinois Press, 1998), 30.

[17] Tice, 111.

[18] Tice, 143.

[19] Tice, 111.

[20] Eleanor Hutzel, "The Policewoman." *The Annals – November 1929.* <http://www.sameshield.com/press/sspress119.html>.
[21] Department of Public Safety, City of Indianapolis, Indianapolis Police Department. "*History: Women and Minorities.*" <http://www.indygov.org/eGov/City/DPS/IPD/About/History/home.htm>.
[22] Walker, 309.
[23] Martha Burk. *The Cult of Power: Sex Discrimination in Corporate America and What Can Be Done About It.* (New York: A Lisa Drew Book/Scribner, 2005), 82.
[24] Kimberly Lonsway, Patricia Aguirre, Nicole Gilliams, et al. "Under Scrutiny: The Effect of Consent Decrees on the Representation of Women in Sworn Law Enforcement." (National Center for Women & Policing, 2003), 2.
[25] Dulaney, 112.
[26] Lonsway, Aguirre, Gilliams et al., 2.
[27] Bureau of Justice Statistics.
[28] Bureau of Justice Statistics.
[29] Jones, 96.
[30] Burk, 17.
[31] Connie Fletcher, *Breaking and Entering: Women Cops Talk About Life in the Ultimate Men's Club.* (New York: HarperCollins Publishers, 1995), 203.
[32] Kenneth Bolton Jr. and Joe R. Feagin, *Black in Blue: African-American Police Officers and Racism.* (New York: Routledge, 2004), 86.
[33] Darlene D. Rogers, "Recruitment and Retention of Minorities and Women in Law Enforcement." (M.A. dissertation, State University of New York Empire State College, 2004), 2-3.
[34] Joe R. Feagin and Hernán Vera, *White Racism: The Basics.* (New York: Routledge, 1995), *ix-x*.
[35] Phylis Chesler, *Mothers on Trial: The Battle for Children & Custody.* (New York: McGraw-Hill Book Co., 1986), 24.
[36] Eve S. Buzawa and Carl G. Buzawa, "Traditional and Innovative Police Responses to Domestic Violence." In *Critical Issues in Policing: Contemporary Readings,* 4th ed., eds. Roger G. Dunham and Geoffrey P. Alpert, 216–237. (Prospect Heights, IL: Waveland Press, 2001), 218.
[37] George Gombossy, "Torrington Suit Held Valid Wives May Sue Police for Protection." *The Hartford Courant,* Oct. 24, 1984. <http://www.jud.state.ct.us/publications/Curriculum/Curriculum7.pdf>.

[38] Anthony V. Bouza, *The Police Mystique: An Insider's Look at Cops, Crime, and the Criminal Justice System*. (New York: Plenum Press, 1990), 210.

[39] Mary Ellen Gale. "Calling in the Girl Scouts: Feminist Legal Theory and Police Misconduct." *Loyola of Los Angeles Law Review*, 34 (2001), 725.

[40] Kappeler, Sluder & Alpert, 292.

[41] Paula S. Rothenberg, Nicolaus Schafhausen and Caroline Schneider, *Race, Class & Gender in the United States: An Integrated Study*, 5th ed. (New York: Worth Publishers, 2000), 131.

[42] Penny Harrington, *Triumph of Spirit*. (Chicago: Britanny Publications, 1999), 25.

[43] Women's Justice Center. "More Sexism Than Ever at Sonoma County Sheriff's Department." <http://www.justicewomen.com/pw_law_suit.html>.

[44] Wendy Austin, "The Socialisation of Women: Male Police Officer Hostility to Female Police Officers." (Paper presented at the Australian Institute of Criminology Conference, First Australasian Women Police Conference. Sydney, Australia, 29–31 July 1996).

[45] "LAPD Working to Get More Female Police Officers." *Los Angeles Times*, May 30, 2003. <http://www.sameshield.com/news/lapd.html>.

[46] Charles R. Swanson, Leonard Territo and Robert W. Taylor, *Police Administration: Structures, Processes, and Behavior*, 5th ed. (Upper Saddle River, NJ: Prentice Hall, 2001), 372.

[47] Robin Morgan, *The Demon Lover: The Roots of Terrorism*. (New York: Washington Square Press, 2001), 23–24.

[48] "LAPD Working to Get More Female Police Officers.

[49] Gale, 733.

[50] John P. Crank, *Understanding Police Culture*. (Cincinnati: Anderson Publishing Co., 1998), 179.

[51] Crank, 182.

[52] Kappeler, Sluder & Alpert, 308-311.

[53] Edwin J. Delattre, *Character and Cops: Ethics in Policing*. (Washington, DC: American Enterprise Institute for Public Policy Research, 2002).

[54] Marilyn Frye, *Politics of Reality: Essays in Feminist Theory*. (Freedom, CA: The Crossing Press, 1983), 4.

[55] Federal Law Enforcement Training Center, "Sexual Discrimination and Sexual Harassment in the Workplace: A Legal Overview." <http://www.fletc.gov/legal/platp/TitleVIIsex.doc>.
[56] Ferrara & Smith.
[57] Ferrara & Smith.
[58] Susan Aaron, "Women with Badges." <http://featuredreports.monster.com/law_enforcement/women/>.
[59] Burk, 65.
[60] White.
[61] Yoshino, xi.
[62] Cynthia Enloe, *Maneuvers: The International Politics of Militarizing Women's Lives*. (Berkeley: University of California Press, 2000).
[63] Lundy Bancroft and Jay Silverman, *The Batterer as Parent: Addressing the Impact of Domestic Violence on Family Dynamics*. (Thousand Oaks, CA: Sage Publications, 2002), 25.
[64] Shannon Morrison et al., "An Evidence-Based Review of Sexual Assault Preventive Intervention Programs." (Technical report prepared for National Institute of Justice, 2006.) <www.ncjrs.gov/pdffiles1/nij/grants/207262.pdf>.
[65] Susan E. Martin, "Doing Gender, Doing Police Work: An Examination of the Barriers to the Integration of Women Officers." (Paper presented at the Australian Institute of Criminology Conference, First Australasian Women Police Conference. Sydney, Australia, 29–31 July 1996).
[66] Ferrara & Smith.
[67] Ferrara & Smith.
[68] Debran Rowland, *The Boundaries of Her Body: The Troubling History of Women's Rights in America*. (Naperville, IL: Sphinx Publishing, 2004), 630.
[69] Jerome H. Skolnick and James J. Fyfe, *Above the Law: Police and the Excessive Use of Force*. (New York: The Free Press, 1993), 96.
[70] Bancroft & Silverman, 7.
[71] Rosanne Cash & Rodney Crowell, "Real Woman." In *Interiors*, Columbia/Legacy compact disc 82876776382, 1990.
[72] Leanor Boulin Johnson, "Burnout and Work and Family Violence Among Police: Gender Comparisons." In *Domestic Violence by Police Officers*, ed. D.C. Sheehan. (Washington, DC: U.S. Department of Justice, 2000), 109.

[73] Leanor Boulin Johnson, Michael Todd and Ganga Subramanian, "Violence in Police Families: Work-Violence Spillover." *Journal of Family Violence*, 20 (2005): 3–12, 7.

[74] Bancroft & Silverman, 3.

[75] James J. Fyfe, Greene et al. *Police Administration*, 5th ed. (New York: McGraw-Hill, 1997), 44.

[76] Frye, 55-56.

[77] Lesley Irving, "Abused Women – Experiences of the Criminal Justice System." <http://www.changeweb.org.uk/abused_women.htm>.

[78] Family Violence Prevention Fund, "Domestic Violence Is a Serious, Widespread Social Problem in America: The Facts." <http://www.endabuse.org/resources/facts/>.

[79] Bancroft & Silverman, 8.

[80] Victor Kappeler, "Kentucky's Response to the Lautenberg Act: Curbing Domestic Violence Among Police." <http://www.lawenforcement.eku.edu/Kjsrb/FEBRUARY99.html>.

[81] Ed Meyer, Kim Hone-McMahan and Keith McKnight, "Few Lose Jobs." *Akron Beacon Journal*, Dec. 5, 1999, A1.

[82] Boulin Johnson, Todd & Subramanian, 3.

[83] Kimberly Lonsway, Diane Wetendorf and Pete Conis, "Lessons Learned from Tacoma: The Problem of Police Officer Domestic Violence." *Law Enforcement Executive Forum* 3 (2003), 28.

[84] John M.A. Violanti, "Partnership Against Police Domestic Violence: The Police and Health Care Systems." In *Domestic Violence by Police Officers*, ed. D.C. Sheehan. (Washington, DC: U.S. Department of Justice, 2000), 355.

[85] G. Terry Bergen, Christine Bourne-Lindamood and Sarah Brecknock, "Incidence of Domestic Violence Among Rural and Small Town Law Enforcement Officers." In *Domestic Violence by Police Officers*, ed. D.C. Sheehan. (Washington, DC: U.S. Department of Justice, 2000), 70.

[86] Michale A. Campion, "Small Police Departments and Police Officer-Involved Domestic Violence: A Survey in Domestic Violence by Police Officers." In *Domestic Violence by Police Officers*, ed. D.C. Sheehan. (Washington, DC: U.S. Department of Justice, 2000), 125.

[87] Robin Klein and Constance Klein, "The Extent of Domestic Violence Within Law Enforcement: An Empirical Study." In *Domestic Violence by Police Officers*, ed. D.C. Sheehan. (Washington, DC: U.S. Department of Justice, 2000), 231.

[88] Boulin Johnson, Todd & Subramanian, 10.
[89] Violanti, 355.
[90] Diane Wetendorf, Interview on *National Public Radio (WBEZ). All Things Considered.* (March 4, 1996).
[91] James Bovard, "The Latest Gun Control Fiasco." <http://www.fff.org/freedom/0597d.asp>.
[92] Meyer, Hone-McMahan & McKnight.
[93] Lonsway, Wetendorf & Conis, 31.
[94] Lonsway, Wetendorf & Conis, 30.
[95] Walker, 326.
[96] Anthony V. Bouza, *Police Unbound: Corruption, Abuse, and Heroism by the Boys in Blue.* (New York: Prometheus Books, 2001), 23.
[97] Victor Kappeler, Richard D. Sluder and Geoffrey P. Alpert, *Forces of Deviance: Understanding the Dark Side of Policing.* (Prospect Heights, IL: Waveland Press, 1994), 75.
[98] Jeff Rojek, Allen E. Wagner and Scott H. Decker, "Addressing Police Misconduct: The Role of Citizens Complaints." In *Critical Issues in Policing: Contemporary Readings,* 4th ed., eds. Roger G. Dunham and Geoffrey P. Alpert. (Prospect Heights, IL: Waveland Press, 2001), 320.
[99] Human Rights Watch, *Shielded from Justice: Police Brutality and Accountability in the United States.* (New York: Human Rights Watch, 1998), 63.
[100] Women Deputies of the Sonoma County Sheriff's Department, "Letter to Sheriff Cogbill." (Dec. 22, 2004). <http://www.justicewomen.com/cc_letter_to_department.pdf>.
[101] Ferrara & Smith.
[102] Ferrara & Smith.
[103] Bancroft & Silverman, 28.
[104] Florida Law Enforcement and Police News, "The Garrity Warning." <www.flacops.com/Garrity-Warning.htm>.
[105] Human Rights Watch, 76.
[106] Bancroft & Silverman, 12.
[107] Violence Policy Center, "American Roulette: Murder-Suicide in the United States." (Washington, DC: Violence Policy Center, 2006.) <http://www.vpc.org/studies/amroul2006.pdf>, 5.
[108] Violence Policy Center, 8.
[109] National Center for Women & Policing, *Recruiting and Retaining Women: A Self-Assessment Guide for Law Enforcement.* (Los Angeles: Feminist Majority Foundation, 1999), 149.

[110] Women Deputies of the Sonoma County Sheriff's Department.

[111] David Burnham, *Above the Law: Secret Deals, Political Fixes, and Other Misadventures of the U.S. Department of Justice.* (New York: Scribner, 1996), 262.

[112] Walker, 278.

[113] Burnham, 68.

[114] Burnham, 361.

[115] Rowland, 604.

[116] Rowland, 604.

[117] Rowland, 600.

[118] Sara Catania, "The Counselor." *Mother Jones,* 30 (2005), 46.

[119] Catharine A. MacKinnon, *Feminism Unmodified: Discourses on Life and Law.* (Cambridge: Harvard University Press, 1987), 16.

[120] Arch Puddington, "The Extent of Police Brutality Is Exaggerated." In *Police Brutality: Opposing Viewpoints,* ed. Helen Cothran. (San Diego: Greenhaven Press, 2004), 43.

[121] Bouza, *Police Unbound,* 23.

[122] Bouza, *Police Unbound,* 25.

[123] National Center for Women & Policing, *Recruiting and Retaining Women: A Self-Assessment Guide for Law Enforcement.*

[124] Joseph D. McNamara, "Police Corruption Is Widespread." In *Police Brutality: Opposing Viewpoints,* ed. Helen Cothran. (San Diego: Greenhaven Press, 2001), 39.

[125] Morgan, *xiii.*

About the Author

Diane Wetendorf is an advocate, trainer and consultant specializing in police-perpetrated domestic violence. With over 20 years experience, she has counseled thousands of women, and provided technical assistance to advocates and law enforcement. Currently a consultant to the Battered Women's Justice Project, Diane is the author of *When the Batterer Is a Law Enforcement Officer: A Guide for Advocates*; *Police Domestic Violence: A Handbook for Victims*; *Abusive Police Officers: Working the System*; *Advocate and Officer Dialogues: Police-Perpetrated Domestic Violence*, and the "Police Power and Control Wheel."

Diane has presented at the National Center for Women and Policing, the International Association of Chiefs of Police, the Behavioral Science Unit of the FBI National Academy, state domestic violence coalitions, and numerous seminars and conferences. She has served as expert witness in the U.S. and Canada. Her website is www.abuseofpower.info.

For more information on obtaining training, technical assistance, or consultation, please contact Diane at (847) ~~749-2560~~ or e-mail dwetendorf@dwetendorf.com.
469.8497

Selected Publications

Police Domestic Violence: A Handbook for Victims (booklet)

As the victim of a police officer, your situation is very different than that of other domestic violence victims. If you have ever tried to get help, you may have become discouraged because no one seemed to understand your plight. Thousands of women who are also in your situation have shared their experiences and helped us write this book.

Advocate & Officer Dialogues: Police-Perpetrated Domestic Violence (booklet)

The tremendous power and authority granted to officers to protect the public can lead to the abuse of their power. Solutions good from the department's perspective can make things worse for the victim; and solutions better for the victim can leave the department open to liability.

Abusive Police Officers: Working the System (booklet)

Police authority, training and the police culture can be used by abusive officers in intimate relationships to bolster their power and control over their victims. Their professional credibility and training uniquely position officers who batter to explain, defend and summon institutional support and assistance from the very systems to which victims are supposed to turn to for help.

Crossing the Threshold: Female Officers and Police-Perpetrated Domestic Violence (softcover)

It is always a volatile situation when a police officer is the perpetrator of domestic violence. It is an explosive situation when both the perpetrator and victim are officers.

To purchase additional books and to stay current, visit our Website at:

http://www.abuseofpower.info

You can also write to Diane Wetendorf at dwetendorf@dwetendorf.com.